Moving Ur

2020 and

Real Life Secrets for Getting from Here to There

3rd Edition

Including Stories from over 30 of the Industry's Top Leaders

John Solleder
with
Keith Hooper

Foreword by

Tracey C. Jones

Moving Up: 2020 and Beyond, 3rd Edition

Published by:
Tremendous Leadership
P.O. Box 267
Boiling Springs, PA 17007
717-701-8159   800-233-2665
www.TremendousLeadership.com

ISBN: 978-1-949033-16-8

Printed in the United States of America

Acknowledgments

Thanks to all the great people who took the time to answer a few short, yet profound, questions about themselves and their multi-level marketing (MLM) business. Some went even further and shared some of the things they have overcome to be a success story. Some are youngsters only a few short years in the industry but are excelling in their companies and being beacon lights for other young folks trying to find their way. Some are old pro's still leading and showing the way after decades in the industry. Some have overcome unique hardships, be they economic or even worse, self-doubt. Some have fought demons that have come their way in the form of alcohol or drug dependency, and spit in the face of these evils and won. And some backed into their business because they found a unique product and just wanted to share it. Some are men and some are women; some speak English, some Spanish, some French, and some multiple languages. All have one thing in common—a desire to embrace the free enterprise system and take care of their families as they see fit via MLM. All are champions. All are winners. All have my utmost respect and love. Enjoy their stories and be inspired!!!

SPECIAL THANKS

To the thousands of courageous people who have worked hard for—and bled for—a better life through MLM, this book is for you. It is about the love affair many of us have with this industry. The MLM industry freed us from the bondage of working for others, giving us a way out of the ghetto, a bad relationship, or worse. For some of us, it gave us a voice to lead and help others and to do what needed to be done; to produce a better world. I still see MLM as the last bastion of free enterprise—the only industry that gives a fighting chance to people willing to work hard, bleed for principle, and develop a mantle of leadership that attracts others needing to be free. Our message is important and urgent. In a troubled economy, these concepts can help people develop the skill set to create new, or even part-time careers, keeping the proverbial wolf from the door.

A MANTLE OF LEADERSHIP

Many people who haven't achieved success wonder why we do what we do? I wrote the first *Moving Up* book in 2005—what seems like an eternity ago. Two of my kids were still in diapers at the time. I wrote the second book in 2011, the year I celebrated my 50th birthday. Yet through all those years,

Acknowledgments

I never realized what the mantle of leadership was until now. When you have thousands of people who know you because of MLM, you become a leader of sorts for many things. One of my children had a challenge with addiction. I chose to share our story with thousands of Facebook followers and had literally hundreds of people praying for her within hours (the power of networking when it really matters). Some people questioned why I would share something so personal. First, I shared because of the mantle of leadership. John F. Kennedy said, "To whom much is given, much is expected." He was right. I've been given a special life because of what I have done for a living. If people knew that even top people can go through this horror, if something like this happens to them, they know they are not alone. They are loved as well. Never be too proud to ask for help and prayerful support.

Second, one of the things we are all taught is the power of association (both good and bad). Our child made a bad choice in one of her associations. That bad choice led to drugs. We asked questions prior but when it all came out our worst suspicions were proven correct. Yet, we were always told everything was "under control." Well, of course, it wasn't. So, here's a non-MLM lesson for parents.

Ask hard questions. Don't try to be your child's friend. You are their parents. We learned this the hard way. The mantle of leadership I've earned will help me provide this message for the rest of my days and hopefully beyond. If you sense your kid is getting involved with bad people, ACT! Don't wait. Our daughter was lucky, and while never truly out of the woods, she was saved and is making every effort to practice sobriety. She has a lifelong road ahead of her. Better to avoid the problem by acting early; if they hate you now, they'll thank you later, God willing.

FOREWORD

As the daughter of Charlie "Tremendous" Jones, I grew up going to numerous network marketing conventions. These events exposed me to the infectious energy of collaborative groups of exuberant people, wise speakers who didn't just talk the talk—but actually walked the walk, and revealed the promise of financial freedom coupled with a lifetime of helping others. My father always told me I had two choices in life, I could either work for someone else, or I could work for myself. It took me decades to realize this, but he was right. I spent years in numerous JOBs before I had to unleash my entrepreneurial side—and I've never looked back.

When John Solleder and Keith Hooper approached me about publishing the 3rd edition of Moving Up 2020, it brought back great feelings of accompanying my father on his speaking trips where I would learn from and with people like them. I knew this book would contain some tremendous truths, but I had no idea just how much these principles applied to anyone, in any industry, at any stage of their life.

John and Keith remind us that free enterprise is the only system of commerce that truly keeps each of us free! This country is built on individuals who possessed a growth mindset, not just for themselves, but for everyone in their orbit. And who better to learn about growing your own business and wealth than John, who has had his hands and head invested in so many different opportunities and his heart committed to the success of so many different individuals.

If you want to learn how to grow your business, get this book. The authors weave interviews through each chapter from people just like you and me who have made the decision to go "all-in." These principles apply to any product or distributorship because the focus is on understanding why direct sales a viable and attainable path to financial freedom and the tools necessary to be successful.

I'm in the publishing and speaking world and my team is excited to read this so we can dial in our prospects, hone our daily method of operations (DMO) and monetize our multiple streams of income (MSI). It's never too late to be what you've always dreamed of. And if you're like me, it may take a couple of decades before it finally sinks in, that you shouldn't dread Monday mornings or feel like your soul was being sucked out of your body. Now is the time for moving up! If you're open and you're willing and you're hungry, please dive right into this book and acquire all the tools you'll need to start the most tremendous chapter of your life!

Tracey C. Jones
President, Tremendous Leadership

INTRODUCTION

I call network marketing the "last bastion of free enterprise." After almost four decades in this industry, I've come to see direct sales as the only enterprise that willingly opens its doors to anyone, regardless of education level, income bracket, gender, race, and even business experience itself. Network marketing defies any demographic profile. And unlike franchises—another gem in the world of free enterprise—you don't need a million dollars or more to get started. Everyone pays the same few hundred dollars to launch their direct-sales business—from the executive who just got a pink slip to the empty-nester who hasn't worked in twenty years. The path to success flashes green lights for every person willing to do the work.

Way back when I started my first network marketing business, my first teacher was a long-haired hippie construction worker who gave me this priceless nugget of wisdom—this business can be learned. I took that to heart and became the "career student" that I am today. To be successful in this business, you must want to learn, and you have to be willing to keep learning. I can think of no other industry like network marketing that offers you the opportunity to develop real and valuable skills. And like all other businesses, the lessons sometimes take place in the school of hard knocks. All of us will fail from time to time. Your skills and personal spirit are what will inspire you to get up, dust yourself off, and try again.

My early mentors also taught me the value of being a good teacher. Another amazing virtue of this last bastion of free enterprise is that success itself is utterly transparent. My success depends on the success of the people in my downline, so it serves me best to invest in my people and share what I've learned. It's a push-pull environment. You want the lifestyle and kind of success I've built, so I teach you my applied science and strategies, and then you pass that knowledge and wisdom along to your own downline people—along with your own tactics and experience—and so on. Success becomes contagious in this business where there are no secrets.

Consider this book a guide for growing your network marketing business. It is essentially a collection of many of the ideas, strategies, and tactics that I was taught by my mentors, as well as practical applications that I've discovered along my own path to success. Take from this book what works for you—and don't stop there. This is one good source. Learn from other people, even from leaders in other industries, who share their experience and key learning principles. When it comes to moving up, your goal is to grow your business and to grow as a person, and there's plenty of wisdom available to be found on book shelves, in lecture halls, and even from your audio player while you're driving your car.

Become a hungry learner! It will serve you well. I wasn't born lucky, and I wasn't an overnight success. I started out a willing and eager student of this industry, and even now—close to four decades later—listening to business-related or personal empowerment CDs is part of my routine every single day. My wife and my three kids depend on me to provide for them, and that means that they depend on me to be the kind of person I have become in the direct-sales business—a businessman who is also a perpetual learner, a teacher and mentor willing to provide my downline with answers to all reasonable questions, and a good person in an industry that provides value for lots of people.

I was asked recently about life values, and during the conversation, I called free enterprise a virtue. Free enterprise is perhaps the most important freedom we have. We need to treasure it and to exercise it, or we'll lose it, along with any right to complain. The network marketing industry is preserving this important freedom more than any other business in the world today. That's why I encourage you to believe in your direct-sales business and to spread the word. Expose your children to it so that they learn the value of free enterprise. Free enterprise leaves you free to "share the wealth," literally and figuratively.

The truth is that by building your network marketing business, you are contributing to job creation. You are helping to educate the children of your distributors by giving them an opportunity to earn an income. You are contributing to society by paying taxes on your earnings to build better schools, roads, and infrastructure. Your direct-sales business is vital to the entire well-being of the planet by bringing life-changing products or services that offer people more value than anything else they could spend their hard-earned money on. Therefore I wrote this book—to share the wealth of what I've learned as I have made my journey to success in direct sales.

Get ready to start moving up! As I stated earlier, I began the Moving Up series in 2005 and added a second edition in 2011. This final edition is Moving Up 2020. The concepts haven't changed. Some of the stories are new and different. Also, because many interviews were done at an earlier time, please keep in mind that the words MLM and network marketing (NM) are interchangeable. Use a highlighter and make notes. After almost four decades I learned a great deal doing these interviews. Great people!

John Solleder

PRAISE FOR JOHN SOLLEDER

"In our business lives we meet people every day who are masters at finding one's Achilles heel and exploiting that weakness to their own advantage. And then we meet people like John Solleder, who see our greatness and encourage us to become the best we can be. John has an innate ability—based on years of experience—to help you create a powerful vision and a path to follow to accomplish your goals. John is not just a nuts and bolts trainer but also a mentor who teaches you how to create relationships that dramatically enhance your life forever. He understands how hard to push, but he also knows how to back off and just be a good friend. John has been a mentor and a great inspiration to me." - **Wally Kralik** continues to lead by example by constantly sponsoring leaders after 23 years with his current company.

"I have watched John from a distance when he was building sales of a competitive company in

Canada. I realized then that he was a guy I could learn from as well as needed to know better. The past 24 years I have watched him as his upline grew and watched him go through every economic cycle, changes in his life as well as even changes in owner-ship and he has always had the proper response. A true GIANT of a man in our industry. In an industry of many GOATS, John is actually one who has risen to the top in every company and has done so for four decades." - **Keith Hooper**

"John Solleder is a network marketing giant who has devoted four decades to developing leaders in the way they should be developed. John 'talks the talk' and 'walks the walk' and has helped thou-sands of people become financially independent. I am one of the fortunate recipients of his generosity and wisdom. John's fundamental success principles are what set him apart, and this book is a must-read if you are looking to find success through network marketing." - **Foster Owusu** came from Africa at a young age with nothing and has inspired thousands of people with his charisma, leadership, and work ethic to not let past circumstances dictate future results. He is a great leader and is building a huge business around the world with his current com-pany. Foster is also the author of "Fire your Boss, Hire Yourself."

"John Solleder is a genuine legend in our indus-try. He has tremendous leadership skills as well as a keen understanding of how to take a product to the marketplace. He is also a master at developing systems and tools that anyone can implement. I have learned an incredible amount from him over the past 32 years that we have been close friends. In terms of business in general and network marketing in particular; he is a true champion!" - **Jeff Weisberg** is a leader in opening markets around the world.

"John Solleder has been my friend and mentor from the time I was a young, single mom struggling to pay bills. Today I'm financially free because of some of the concepts he teaches. Listen to this guy. I did, and it was the best business decision I made to date." - **Karen Ford**

"John has been my friend and amazing mentor since 1989, when I first met him at a meeting in Toronto. I heard about how this (then young) guy already achieved great success and he was doing a meeting and I needed to attend. As advertised he spent four hours teaching and another two hours answering questions. I never saw someone with his stamina to help people in my business. We've been friends ever since and shared many happy moments and a few sad ones. He's family to me." - **Arlene Lowy**

"I have known John since the early 1990s as a friend and colleague. He has always been there for me and my teams and is always willing to answer questions, get on calls, and even fly across the ocean to help my teams in Europe. After almost 40 years, he's still getting the job done at a high level." - **Don Hutchinson**

Table of Contents

Chapter 1

IN THE BEGINNING

The year was 1983. The economy is having the wind sucked out of it, and I'm finishing up my undergrad degree at Seton Hall University. My dad was an electrician, and I had spent some of my summers working for him. The foreman was a nice guy, who figured that with my athletic background, I could carry pipe and get coffee. As it turns out, I was reasonably successful at remembering how the journeymen took their coffee, but I had absolutely no aptitude for anything mechanical. Christmas of my senior year in college, my own father fired me. He said that I'd better figure out some other way to make a living because it would never be with my hands.

I was getting my degree in communications, so I thought I'd look for a job that involved writing—maybe in advertising or marketing. Not long into the job search, I realized that I was essentially qualified to do next to nothing. In the spring of my senior year, I was working part time at a health club and ran into Tom Husted, a friend I had wrestled with in college. I asked Tom what he was up to, and he mentioned a company I had never heard of in something called network marketing.

He said that another recent college grad from our area had started with the same company a few years before and was already earning over $6,000 a month. That guy's name was Mark Zuckerbrod, and he was doing a meeting a few nights later if I'd like to check it out. Six thousand dollars was a bunch of money for a broke college kid looking for his first real job. Tom told me that I could get started for thirty-two dollars, so I wrote him a "bouncy" check and begged him to hold onto it until payday at the gym.

My parents' reaction was less than enthusiastic. They insisted that I had been conned into a pyramid scheme. It was a big disappointment to them to think of their soon-to-be-college-graduate son selling vitamins. But there I was, $30,000 in debt from student loans, with no other prospects for a career. I figured I might as well see what these people could tell me about making money. That night, I read the career manual from cover to cover. I filled up a couple of yellow pads with notes, diagrams, and equations. I wrote out the names of all the people I knew and attached dollar amounts to each name. And by about 4.00 a.m. I had earned my first million, just on the people I already knew. I thought: This business is going to be a piece of cake. And wouldn't everyone see what I saw? (P.S. It was much easier on paper).

I guess it was easy to think that way before I had sponsored my first person or retailed my first nutrition program. The next day I called my brother-in-law, who had an MBA. I figured that he knew lots of people and would be a good prospect. He told me that he had joined one of those network marketing things once upon a time and that I'd see the error of my ways when I got older. For now, I should listen to my parents and get a regular job. I was bummed. I called my friend, Eric, who also said I was nuts, but he had a friend named Peter who might be interested because Peter wanted to lose weight. That weekend, Tom Husted and I met with Peter and Eric. Peter got excited, and both he and Eric joined—and Peter purchased $800 worth of product. Even though I hadn't really earned any money yet, at that point I knew I was going to make it. Come hell or high water, I would make it!

In the Game

You see, over the previous five years, I had been through the ringer: major spinal surgery, the death of two very close friends in automobile accidents, and the passing of my Uncle James, who had helped to raise me, at age fifty-one. Making money seemed so much less complicated than dealing with those situations. I thought about the book my father had shared with me while I was hospitalized for the spinal surgery, "The Power of Positive Thinking," by Dr. Norman Vincent Peale. I will never forget Dr. Peale's sage advice, "If you think you have problems, go to a nursing home or funeral parlor." The great preacher couldn't have been more right. Earning a living has its challenges, but at least you know that you are in the game—alive and kicking—and eventually you'll figure it out.

The next defining moment came at my college commencement ceremony at Seton Hall. My academic education was ending that day, but fortunately for me, my entrepreneurial education was just starting. I'd grown up in a home where "business owners" were looked on with suspicion. My parents were strong advocates of unions and workers' rights, and the conversation was always about the wealthy versus the folks who worked for them. To say that my parents were staunch members of the Democratic Party would be an understatement! My Dad lived by mottos such as, "Buy American, Buy Union" and "A fair day's work for a fair day's pay." So, when Seton Hall invited President Reagan to be our commencement speaker, I said flat out that they could mail me my degree. No way was I going to sit and listen to that union buster and turncoat who had once been president of the Screen Actors' Guild.

But my father said that I had to go, if for no other reason than to show respect for the presidential office. As it turned out, the "great communicator" had a life-changing message for me. He talked about how he'd graduated at the height of the Depression and how he had no idea what he was going to do besides being a lifeguard. He spoke about freedom in terms of what it meant to be a free person in a free entrepreneurial society. What former President Reagan said at the end of his speech is what got me. He quoted an old businessman who had survived the Great Depression and who told him, "Look, maybe I could get someone to give you a job, but they would only be doing it because I asked. They wouldn't have a real interest in you. Instead, go knock on a lot of doors and find someone who takes an interest in teaching you. It doesn't matter the industry or business. Find the thing that someone will teach you and pursue it." Get a mentor. That was priceless advice.

Ready to Learn, Ready to Change

Around this time, I heard about a meeting that the vice president of marketing for my new network marketing business was doing in Hartford. I invited four people to go with me and, because cash was tight, the five of us shared a hotel room. The passion of the event, the excitement of the industry, and the realization that maybe we had all found a better way in a tough economy made it easy to sleep on the floor and eat peanut butter sandwiches all weekend. We were young nomads on a mission to change the world and, most importantly, to change ourselves.

The information shared with us that weekend just kept getting better. After a few hours of speeches from local leaders, the man of the hour, Lawrence Thompson, was introduced. I have never seen Elvis perform, but I imagine that his concerts must have felt something like this. When they introduced "LT," smoke started billowing out from everywhere, and balloons streamed from the ceiling. It was like a rock concert and political rally rolled into one. Now, I can't tell you everything that I learned that day, but three major gems have stuck with me to this day:

- Anyone can learn this industry, if they apply themselves.

- This is a benevolent business: What you learn is only valuable if you teach others.

- "For things to change, you have to change, and for things to get better, you have to get better." (This is the now-famous statement LT made that day.) (It was another powerful phrase I believe he had learned from the great Jim Rohn).

We made it back to New Jersey in what seemed like minutes, propelled by the message of change. I started to look at myself differently. "Change what?" I asked myself. Well, my attitude about money for one thing! I needed to realize that money is good and has immense power, as long as it is earned honorably and used to help others as well as myself. I also needed to change my attitude about my own ability to succeed— despite my parents and other well-intentioned people telling me that this crazy idea wasn't going to work for me. I had to overcome such statements as

- "You're too young."

- "You don't have the right contacts."

- "You're getting into the company too late."
- "You have no money to live on while you do the business."
- "You have an education from a great university, so why would you want to be a vitamin salesman?"

Most of the people trying to tell me not to go into direct sales as a profession, were not going to the meetings I attended, seeing the people I saw, or gathering the information I was getting on the network marketing business. I knew that I would need to make this business my own. I quickly realized that if I were to become more and get more out of life, I'd have to establish a few guidelines. I've applied them to my own business and have been sharing them with my downline ever since. Here they are:

The Leading Producers in Your Business are Like Your Family

They are the reason you have a check from your company. Always do everything possible to help them grow. Their success is your success, so make every effort to support their growth. Focus more on your people earning income than on your own income, and you can't help but succeed.

Another couple who started their careers in the network marketing industry back in the early 1980s and are still going strong are Don and Pam

Hutchinson from Spain. Here's a recent interview you'll find of interest.

Over 30 years ago, when Pam and I were introduced to network marketing by a friend, we saw the possibilities; to create a business enterprise of our own, to work at our own pace, to learn the "how-tos" as we took our early steps, and to have a trusted friend as a mentor. As a self-employed salesperson and a bank clerk, the concept of recurring income to secure our financial future was compelling.

For us the benefits of the product were paramount. As Pam often said when told she was a great salesperson, her response was, "I'm not a salesperson, I believe in the product!" There are those for whom the financial reward is more important than the quality or benefits of the product or service. That's ok. We all have different priorities. Our view is that an organization can best grow through personal recommendation when there is a strong product or service at its core. A good question to ask yourself is: "Would I continue to buy this product/service if there was no financial opportunity attached to it?" If the answer is "yes," you have a solid foundation for you to build a sustainable business.

As we learned, one of the biggest advantages from this business is 'choice.' When you have available a wider selection of quality choices than before, life can be more fulfilling. It can be, but taking advantage of those opportunities is up to you. As well as facing challenges and improving our skills and disciplines, we enjoyed the development of new relationships with like-minded people; the fun of friendship, not worrying about paying for our three sons to have an excellent high level education, travelling to all the continents of the world, choosing to support charities as well as establishing our own charitable foundation, being open and willing to learn from great mentors, celebrating success and also looking in the mirror when things were not going as well as we thought they should. Facing adversity and overcoming it contrasted with the challenge of dealing with prosperity and how to deal sensibly with that.

We certainly did make mistakes!

Learning from those mistakes enabled us to do better and to pass our experiences and techniques to others. One of the great joys you will experience as you progress is seeing others succeed.

It's been said that a person who never made a mistake, never made anything! So it's not important what happens to you, but it is important how you deal with it and what you learn from those situations.

Finally, get going, keep going and, in the words of one of our great mentors, "have a burning desire, be teachable and be willing to go to work.

Learn and Apply the 80-15-5 Formula

About 80 percent of the people in your group are part-time people. Spend 5 percent of your time working with them. Another 15 percent of your group is in growth mode today. Spend 80 percent of your time working with them. The final 5 percent of your group are in maturity mode and are your top check earners. Spend 15 percent of your time helping them grow. Don't forget that the 15 percent in growth mode are today's new growing business. If you want your check to grow, focus on today's growing business.

Invest in Your Business

Distributorships are not much different from traditional franchise businesses. The major difference is that the startup cost for a direct-sales distributorship is tiny by comparison. However, if you want to be successful, you need to acquire the attitude and commitment of a franchisee and invest time and some money in marketing to get things going. Remember that you are limited only by your vision of how large you desire to be.

This Business Is Not for Everyone

One of my early reality checks was discovering that not everyone saw what I saw in this business. That's okay. There are enough people out there who will see what you see.

Aim for Greatness

As I look back over my almost 40 years as a high-income earner in the network marketing industry, I measure my success not in dollars earned but in the value of my life experiences. Earning money while visiting the Holy Land. Spending time in Israel, Jordan, and Egypt. Building downlines in Australia, New Zealand, Japan, Hong Kong, Germany, Belgium, Holland, the United Kingdom, Ireland, Italy, Spain, India, Trinidad, and Tobago, as well as in great new markets like Guatemala, Colombia, Peru, and Ecuador. Most recently, I spent several weeks in Iceland, a country that seems like a postcard on every street. I meet great people in great markets. The world gets much smaller under the umbrella of free enterprise!

Hilda Olavarietta is a perfect example of one of the many people who embraces network marketing and is making a great career of it. Here's some of her story.

In the year 2000, after a difficult financial situation, I got a check from a company whose products I was using and recommending to my family. The check was the bonus money from consuming the product and making recommendations.

There the penny dropped, and I thought... if this company that I do not dedicate time to is sending me money, what would happen if I spent that time building my own business?

I gave up my traditional work, which was good, and I thought I had a good salary, but not time or enough freedom to get out of my commitments and fulfill my dreams. Thank God the decision was right, in a short time my new income greatly exceeded what I earned in traditional work, and this has allowed me to fulfill many dreams and I'm still going for more.

I love my job. I'm happy.

What has the industry done for you and your family?

I can be free, own my own business, give my children the ability to attend good schools, travel to extraordinary places with all expenses included, accompanied by wonderful people, help many people to fulfill their dreams, be blessed by people who the system has allowed me to help. Reaching my old age healthy, active and with financial freedom and not depending on anything or anyone.

How is the future looking?

Extraordinary, enjoying life with many dreams still to be fulfilled, surrounded by wonderful people, transcendent, leave a legacy to my family and continue helping to impact the lives of thousands of people.

Every day for me this is just the beginning, a great mission of life.

And the friendships that grow out of this business are invaluable, too. Tom Husted, the guy who got me started in the industry, lives in Thailand, and we keep in contact by e-mail just about every week. People such as Mark Zuckerbrod, Jeff Weisberg, and my first big-time mentor, Larry Thompson, are among my closest friends. And through this business, I met my wife and partner, Josee. After I had been through a painful divorce, a well-meaning distributor (not even in my downline) decided to introduce me to his girlfriend's best friend. Even though we were separated by 2,000 miles, Josee and I eventually married and now have three beautiful children. Now, I'm not suggesting that by getting into network marketing you'll find the love of your life, but you never know.

Foster Owusu is a guy who has become a good friend, and has worked arm in arm with me for the last few years.

What did you do before MLM?

I had pursued a few career paths prior to joining MLM. Some by choice and others by circumstances beyond my control. I was educated in the field of Accountancy. However, after several years of working in the Accounting field in my home country of Ghana, I found it necessary to migrate to Canada in search of better opportunities.

As a new arrival in Canada in the mid-eighties, with zero Canadian experience, I had very few career options. I accepted whatever legal job was available to me, which mostly meant working in the manufacturing industry as a laborer. During that time, I got introduced to a networking opportunity. I liked the approach and the introduction to the freedom enterprise. I saw a light at the end of the tunnel, and I have not looked back since.

What have you overcome in your life to become a success?

There are several things I could mention, but I would rather focus on the number one most important item. There is a saying that "the person who chases two rabbits catches none." Also, "you cannot serve two masters." Case in point – if I was going to succeed, I knew I had to find a good company and stick to it long term.

These lessons were taught to me very early as a child. Therefore, I knew that the biggest, most important thing I had to overcome to become a success is DISTRACTION. I had a clear picture of what I wanted my future to look like. I was willing to make the necessary sacrifices to eliminate any and all distractions.

I knew that the networking opportunity was going to become the vehicle for my exit strategy from the 9-5 routine.

Moving from a paycheck to purposeful living does require a shift in mindset and a shift in heart-set. I did both and I quickly came to the realization that things would have to change. This also meant that the people that I was spending my time with would have to come along or be left behind. The choice was theirs.

How do you see your business as a Multiple Stream of Income (MSI) for others?

The concept of having multiple streams of income in our economy is a no brainer. It takes bundles to live a comfortable life. As a matter of fact, my wife's favorite line when it comes to extra income is simply, "extra means extra!" The idea of job security is nonexistent in this modern era. Therefore, creating multiple streams of income is the smartest thing to do.

What does the future look like?

The reality is that we are all struggling for or with something in life. For some it might be health, for some it might be loneliness, for some it might be money, for some it might be finding a purpose in life to contribute to the greater good.

For me, the present allows me to contribute today in order to have a lasting impact on humanity. I have been blessed in so many different ways, including having an opportunity to contribute to the greater good. My life has meaning, and I am here to leave an imprint by touching lives in a positive way. I want to be the kind of instrument that has a positive influence on society.

End Note

As a personal note, I would like to create a legacy in the financial, business and spiritual arena. I would like to build a sustaining business by creating a pathway for the generations to come. It will sadden me greatly if I am forgotten the day I leave this planet. I hope to leave a lasting mark in the heart and mind of every human being that crosses my path. I have a deep, heartfelt desire to contribute to society in this way – through network marketing I am confident that I will fulfill this dream and thus make my contribution to society.

Dr. Soraya Aguiar is a very talented lady, to say the least. She continues to set monthly records in her company. Another recent interview revealed some of her journey.

What made you see network marketing as a business and in what year?

I came to network marketing in 2011 because of a health challenge, and I stayed for the freedom that I understood residual income could give me.

For many years I practiced my dentistry career with great success, but when I got sick everything stopped and so did the income. I registered as a consultant simply to buy the products at a discount, but after having extraordinary results in my health, I decided to take a closer look at the business and I was passionate about the idea of building a business that would give me economic freedom as well as the freedom of time to travel and enjoy with my family without money being a problem.

What has the industry done for you and your family?

It has given me freedom—that is what I value most in this life, after my family; it has given me options; it has given me the power to choose and design the life I want to live, and not the life I can live.

It allowed me to travel a lot, to know other cultures, wonderful people who have contributed a lot in my life. It has allowed me to share great moments with my family, moments that I used to miss because I had to work. It allowed me to give quality time to my mother when she fell ill, and to be able to cover all her expenses without money being a problem. It has given me the privilege of adding value to the people around me, and above all, it has helped me to have a higher quality relationship with my husband because we do the business together.

How is the future?

I feel very happy and excited about the future, because this industry has allowed me to create security, the security of having a strong economic backup, which allows me to keep my eyes on more transcendental things.

Several of my dreams have already been fulfilled, and others are about to be fulfilled. I have been able to help other people to be more prosperous in an integral way, and that makes me live with purpose, which fills my soul with joy.

One of my main goals is to directly help a thousand women to empower themselves emotionally and financially, so that they in turn do the same with other women. Only this industry can give me the tools I need to be able to carry it out, and here we really fulfill the saying that says "the sky is the limit."

I'll conclude this chapter with an invitation: If you're willing to work hard and truly care about making a difference in this world, then I invite you to read on. I encourage you to let the ideas, strategies, and tactics in this book captivate you. I hope that some of my hard-learned business lessons will help you get to whatever level you aspire to. But I have to say that the best way to learn the network marketing business is to do it. This the last bastion of free enterprise and the best place for average people like you and me to attain greatness.

Chapter 2

MONEY MATTERS

Years ago, I was quoted in a magazine as saying that the purpose of money is to love people. I stand by that statement today. To me, money only has value if it's used to make the world a better place. Whether it is to educate your children, feather your retirement account, or endow your church with new hymnals, there are always plenty of places to use your money. The value lies in its power to bless people.

With that perspective, your bank statements can function as a kind of moral report card. How much did you put away for your children's college fund or your own retirement? Did you move closer to independence from government support or from being a financial burden on your children? Your checkbook register is a telling score sheet—come tax time, we get to see where we stand. Did I contribute to my church or to St. Jude's research? To the Girl Scouts or Boy Scouts or Make A Wish? To disabled vets? Take a look at your checkbook to see who your money has helped this year.

If the answer is nobody, maybe it is time to ask yourself what you are working for.

Being self-employed gives us the freedom to make our money matter. In direct sales, we tend to think that when we sell a product or service, we are creating income for ourselves and our upline. The reality is that our sales success generates countless jobs.

Think about it. Who makes the corrugated boxes your product arrives in? Who prints your brochures and business cards? Who manufactures your product? Who sources the ingredients for your product? What shipping company brings your product to you and your customers? What Internet company provides your back-office system? What lead company sold you your sales leads? You get the picture. Your direct-sales success touches a great many other people's lives. How's that for motivation?

Charity Begins at Home

Of course, we all know that charity begins at home. One of my primary motivators has been the positive impact my career has had on my children. Now 24 years old, my daughter has been in the inspiring company of leaders such as Robert and Kim Kiyosaki, Dr. Dennis Waitley, Zig Ziglar, and myriad other industry gurus. She has been in the audience at many of my lectures on free enterprise, capitalism, and network marketing as a business. My daughter has sat through many a meeting with my attorneys, CPAs, and business colleagues. The exposure to optimistic people and inspiring ideas has shaped her in the very best of ways.

My younger kids have had the same opportunity being around many great leaders from my current company as well as friends in other companies. When our daughter recently went through a major life challenge, she said to me "I know what you're going to say, Dad, 'a day at a time, a brick at a time, process by process is how we're going to beat this thing.'" Interesting the self-development tools we gather along the path.

Another young person who grew up in our current company attending events with his parents is Michael Walper. Michael earned a degree in kinesiology as well as a master's degree in physio-therapy at McGill University. And he is one of our current companies rising stars. While a good college education can be invaluable, it's tough to deny the inherent value of practical work experience. Let's hear it from Michael:

> When I looked for my first real job back in 1983, I learned that despite having a solid education from a fine school, it was the hands-on work experience that proved to be the determining factor in getting hired. All decent direct-selling companies offer training programs. Why not have your children enroll as distributors as early as legally possible? They'll attend classes, read the literature,

listen to the recordings, and acquire strategies that will serve them well in the years ahead.

Anyone who has built a direct-selling business will tell you that it is the ultimate personal development exercise. Nothing is quite like it for challenging one's tenacity—when people don't show up for meetings, when friends and family tell you that you're crazy. But once the confidence kicks in, it brings with it self-sufficiency to last a lifetime. That's a legacy worth passing on.

Michael Walper's parents were ranchers in western Canada for many years when they discovered a little business called network marketing. Working from home with three kids under the age of seven and the nearest neighbor nine miles away, the odds of success were not in their favor. However, Sandi and Carl decided that one way or another they would rock and roll from their ranch to MLM success. Keep in mind that when they started in a very rural area there were no cell phones, fax machines or even some of the computer technology we take for granted today. Yet as young parents with over $250,000 of debt on their ranch, they had to make it. The facts don't matter when your WHY is big enough. Today they have three well-educated children who attended great schools and are writing their own history. Yet without the tenacity shown by their parents early on, they never would have the lives they are living.

The Penny Principle

Part of that legacy is what I call the "penny-saved principle." Einstein was once quoted as saying that his greatest discovery was not any of the things he's famous for, but rather his realization of the power of compound interest. Just for fun, sit down and see what would happen if you took $100 and grew it at 10 percent annually. Extend that compound-interest calculation out over ten years, and the results are staggering. By the end of the seventh year, you have almost doubled your initial $100 investment. And by the end of ten years, you have more than two and a half times your initial investment.

year	Starting Amount	Interest Rate	Interest Earned	Amount at year End *(after Compounding)*
1	$100	10 percent	$10	$110
2	$110	10 percent	$11	$121
3	$121	10 percent	$12.10	$133.10
4	$133.10	10 percent	$13.31	$146.41
5	$146.41	10 percent	$14.64	$161.05
6	$161.05	10 percent	$16.11	$177.16
7	$177.16	10 percent	$17.72	$194.88
8	$194.88	10 percent	$19.49	$214.37
9	$214.37	10 percent	$21.44	$235.81
10	$235.81	10 percent	$23.58	$259.39

Taking an even longer-range view, let's say that you put away $100 a month at a modest 4 percent interest beginning at age 25 and did it consistently for thirty years. You'd have $69,736.29 by the time you hit age fifty-five, and you would have earned $33,636.29 just in interest. You get the idea, and it's probably not the first time you've heard it. And yet, somehow, we aren't teaching our young people the power of compound interest or, more important, the old adage, "A penny saved is a penny earned." Encourage your kids and grandkids to save. It's priceless advice.

Daniella and Cassidy Parlance are leaders in the counseling world who have an inspiring story and include network marketing as a multiple source of income (MSI).

What did you do before MLM?

Before MLM, I had a strong background in aesthetics and make-up artistry. I eventually transitioned into the medical field working as a medical laboratory technician for over ten years. After getting married and having two children back-to-back, we made the decision for me to stay home full time and home school. My husband, Cassidy, works in the trades, is a prison ministry volunteer and a Worship Artist. Together, we authored the book "What Love Is Not" and founded a marriage and music ministry entitled "Make Your Marriage Great Again."

We have always been passionate about the natural and holistic lifestyle and became

intrigued when we came across a revolution-
ary product that boosts the immune system
naturally. This is where our journey with networking began. We started taking a variety
of products from this line. My husband had
transitioned to working twelve hour rotating
shifts and was struggling with low energy
levels during his night shifts. He began feeling a significant difference in his energy levels
and that was when we knew we had to share
it with the world! We decided this was a perfect opportunity to merge the spiritual aspect
of our ministry with physical and financial
health.

We plunged full force into network marketing and will never look back!

*What have you overcome in your life to become a
success?*

As a child, I suffered from a rare debili-
tating anxiety disorder called Selective Mut-
ism. My faith and desire to break free were
my anchor and gave me the strength to overcome. Over the years I still struggled with
social anxiety and saw the patterns of how it
stifled my passion to help people and limited
my life. This was when I decided enough was
enough and started to challenge myself to
take steps to overcome my fears.

I started the healing process by writing about it. This empowered me, and as I

interacted on social media with other people who experienced my pain, I was compelled to finish and release the book years later, entitled "Words of a Mute Girl." The journey was painful, and it only got worse when I entered a long, dysfunctional marriage, and eventually faced a devastating divorce. In my quest for meaning and hope, I had a spiritual encounter that radically transformed my life and renewed my faith in God. About four years later, I met my soulmate, Cassidy.

Interestingly enough, my husband and I share a strikingly similar back story of a failed marriage relationship. It was the darkest experience in both our lives. We also realized this wasn't unique to us, but an increasingly common scenario for so many people. We decided that rather than be defined by our past, we would overcome our shame and insecurities and instead start a movement to empower other couples or people who have been devastated by broken relationships to move forward and succeed.

We have written a book, "What Love Is Not," as a roadmap for successful marriage based on solid biblical principles, statistics and our personal experience. We've since ventured out to become Nouthetic Marriage Counselors to allow us to work with people one-on-one and also build relationships while helping people restore their relationships. In our ministry, we address all different aspects of relationships, including dating, premarital and how to move forward after divorce. We arrange monthly date nights for couples, as well as yearly marriage conferences and workshops throughout the year to empower people to be passionate and purposeful and address the power of the 'why' behind marriage.

How do you see your business as an MSI for others?

Our approach comes from a holistic perspective—body, mind, and spirit. In our quest for further addressing the physical aspects of a healthy relationship, we incorporated an amazing natural product line into our ministry, which we absolutely fell in love with after experiencing results first-hand. The signature product works as a precursor to build the immune system which addresses a root issue.

We believe that our ministry has the unique advantage of allowing us to connect with people at a deep level in two ways; spiritually and practically. We see the network marketing company we are a part of as a bridge because it has offered us a two-tier strategy; the ability to offer both the tools for improving peoples' overall health and wellbeing, as well as the opportunity to improve their financial state.

What does the future look like?

Our vision is to host marriage conferences, seminars and workshops and start a movement to make marriage great again across our province, country and beyond. Marriage ministry is lacking especially in churches today. Our desire is to incorporate our conferences and teachings as virtual courses and bible studies to better equip churches with resources for their congregations.

We plan to get our book, "What Love Is Not," in as many hands as possible, worldwide, and also publish many other books in the works!

Since we joined the network marketing industry, it has opened up our mind to so many valuable resources that are not only applicable to business, but to all areas of life. MLM truly is a gateway to holistic living. It's deeper than just sales. It's about connecting with people at a deeper level. Familiarizing yourself with their pain, their dreams and desires and pulling out the problem solver in you to assist them in addressing their issues. Yes, it has its challenges, but for us, the drive to want to see people succeed and overcome far outweighs all time and effort invested. Because after all, that's how we see it—as an investment in ourselves and others!

Another great guy I've worked with through the years is Jim Spencer. Jim has a great marketing perspective, as he'll now share.

I was first exposed to MLM in the summer of 1991. I was then a professional photographer working in New York City, and my office was 2 blocks from Madison Square Garden. For about 10 years I was the most widely published photographer in the world with books and magazine photography exceeding a billion copies per year. Approaching 40 years of age I was intrigued with the possibilities of leveraging myself in a business that could eventually involve thousands. There had been occasions for me to train assistants in my field of expertise, but it seemed as though once they became proficient with the skills I imparted to them, they went on to open their own businesses and actually became competition.

So, I remember making a decision around 1993 that I would look for the right company and product line for myself. I actually had a measure of success with two different companies before I settled on the one that would become my main focus on a permanent basis. I had a bad experience, though, with both of them, which prompted me to walk away from them even the though the latter of the two was generating over ten thousand dollars a month already. Settling back into the photography world, I stumbled onto the right combination in a company in late 1998. I was looking for the three fundamentals…a product line that everyone needs, nobody else has and is affordable.

The problem was, my immediate circle of associates were not keen on me doing this type of business at all. Because of the previous bad experience, even my wife pressured me to not do it. Against her judgment I had to make an executive decision to go forward.

The first three months working part-time with the new company generated a few thousand dollars, but more importantly it won three all expense tickets on a beautiful cruise ship with a week in the Caribbean. I surprised my wife and young daughter with the trip and after meeting the principals of the company on the cruise my wife acquiesced that she liked the company and the people running it.

Over twenty years later, I look back on the thousands of people I have helped physically and financially with this business. It's true that we have made millions of dollars over the years, but the ability to help so many people in so many ways has made the journey amazing and totally worthwhile.

In the past year we have traveled to several countries to introduce the business concept and product to people who have never seen such things. What a thrill to help people in just a few months exceed their monthly incomes by multiple times, in some cases! Not to mention the many who have been helped physically with the products.

One thing to remember about the direct sales industry...it seems to always be on the cutting edge of scientifically produced products and is usually first to bring them to market. Usually the product cost would be prohibitive through general marketing structures. However, the distributors become the advertising mechanism and greatly reduce costs related to that expense. So, the savings can be passed on to the general public and they can enjoy unique products not readily available.

I have now been involved with the industry for over 28 years and have seen it grow into a juggernaut, moving hundreds of billions of dollars of product each year. I see only growing bigger as time goes on.

While the business is perhaps not for everyone, it can be a viable business for people who are self-starters and want to have early retirement, so they can focus on what they feel are the important things in life.

Cash is King

After almost 40 years as a small-business owner, I have learned from direct experience that a business with cash flow can survive anything, even the devastating economic downturn. There always will be people who come out of a recession ahead of the game for the pure economic reason that if you have cash, you can essentially buy at a discount against the former value of an asset. If the asset returns to—or even exceeds—its prior value, you will have made a nice profit.

So there's another legacy principle—cash truly is king, and the path to financial freedom is all about cash flow. Here's my advice when it comes to maximizing your personal cash flow:

- Learn to pay off the bill with the highest rate of interest first. This means that if you have two bills, one for $5,000 with a fixed rate of 10 percent and the other for $3,000 with a variable rate, currently at 18 percent, you definitely should pay off the $3,000 bill first because it carries higher interest and the risk of a varying rate.

- Use the tax system to maximize deductions while paying off anything that is not tax favored first. For example, a few years ago I used a life insurance loan to invest in several business ventures. I also used a home equity loan to do some home remodeling. The rates on both loans were about the same. However, since I could not deduct the use of the insurance money in the same way as I could deduct the home equity funds, I paid off the insurance loan first.

- Learn to maximize retirement savings. While I am not licensed to give financial advice, I will say that if your government allows for deductions against your income for contributing to an individual retirement account (IRA), why not take full advantage of it? Examine long-term care insurance for yourself and your spouse so as not to be a burden on your kids if you are put in a long-term care situation.

David and Catharine Haire, another great couple I've known for the last few years, come from the financial world. They live in a unique part of the world I've grown to enjoy as well, in the North of Ireland.

We have been in MLM for four years and use it as an MSI.

We currently run a successful financial services business and overseas property company. We meet many successful people who are always interested in better health and many are also interested in upping their income.

We see a great future in MLM for ourselves and family. We see MLM becoming our main source of income in the future and well into retirement.

Everyone should consider MLM, as anyone can do it. You don't need to invest money, but you do need to invest time. MLM is something that can be done part time without affecting your existing commitments. The income you receive is unlimited. You get paid exactly for your effort. You are building a legacy for your family. So, find your own reason and purpose and GO DO IT! You owe it to yourself and family.

Either let someone else hire your skills and talent and get a "job" or develop your own entrepreneurial skills through MLM and get paid what you are worth. For us MLM just made much more sense.

Practice Makes Permanent

My favorite legacy principle is a twist on the one our mothers taught us. Practice might not always make perfect—we all know that perfection is rare—but it makes permanent. Let's say that you sleep on the right side of your bed at home. Chances are that you'll sleep on the right side of the bed when you're on the road, too. We all get grooved into our habits, and what we practice does indeed become permanent for all of us.

I'm a big fan of amateur wrestling. When my friend, Brandon Slay, won a gold medal for wrestling in the 2000 Sydney Olympics, he defeated a former Olympic champion and a many-time world champion from the Soviet Union. As a dedicated student of his opponent's moves, Brandon intently studied his Russian counterpart's moves. In preparation for his own match with the Soviet wrestler, Brandon rehearsed his countermoves mentally thousands of times. His practice became permanent. So much so that when it came time to face his opponent, Brandon instinctively anticipated the Soviet's moves, countered them successfully, and took the championship.

What about the captain of that 2009 flight that was hit by birds as it took off from LaGuardia Airport? When interviewed afterwards, Captain "Sully" Sullenberger said that he had spent his entire career preparing for an unlikely moment like that one. All the years of practice had forged permanent reflexive piloting skills that saved Sully's life and the lives of 155 passengers.

Whether wrestling, piloting a commercial airliner, or sharing your network marketing business opportunity—practice does make permanent. When that promising recruit is within your grasp, the countless hours of preparation will meet with the opportunity, and your income will show the results.

One of the great blessings in our industry is some of the people you meet. The life stories and how they got involved in MLM are always of interest. That being the case, we wanted to ask a few of the many great people we have come to know what led them to get involved. I'm a guy with many military members in my family and I have great regard for those selfless enough to put themselves in harm's way for freedom. This next lady is one such hero of mine.

Meet Suzette McKay. I remember meeting Suzette and her husband, Moses, in Toronto when she was recently out of the military and had been a customer of one of my downlines. She was a well-educated lady who had an amazing life story. I have great respect for the military and we became, and still are, friends. We flew on a puddle jumper from Victoria, BC to Vancouver, and it was the scariest 12 minutes of my life. But I knew if anything went wrong, she would get out and fix that plane mid-air—that's the level of confidence she possesses.

What caused you to look at Network Marketing?

I am a retired aircraft technician who served with the Royal Canadian Air Force and was actually never introduced to this business model till I was in my 40s. I came to the industry looking to purchase a consumable lifetime product at a wholesale price for health reasons. They explained there was an opportunity for a part-time or full-time income with capabilities of me setting my own hours or goals. This was extremely enticing. My first goal was to get enough income to consume unlimited product. Goals and dreams grew with income.

When I was explained the numbers and benefits of leveraging time and effort of many people, an understanding came that this was a win-win situation, as well as a very inspiring business model for all involved. I was astounded and wondered why anyone would follow a traditional business with staffing problems, little flexibility, and major overhead.

What has it done for you?

It has given me the freedom to earn money on my own terms. I can work lots or a little when other priorities take precedence. It has given me the ability to move across the country because of a family situation and still continue to grow. Our household residual income from network marketing is a great deal more than our hard-earned income from military pensions and was earned in far less time. My MLM paycheck continues to grow exponentially, where my pension won't ever grow. The gifts that come from helping others, choosing to work with others who are fun and inspiring, mixed with opportunities for self-development are just a few of the numerous benefits.

Where do you see it going?

The industry is growing by leaps and bounds and is currently surmounting every other global industry. Demand for less commuting, the flexibility of work hours from home and unlimited income ceilings are in high demand. Fear of living longer, outgrowing our retirement savings and the desire for long-term residual income are ever-increasing factors. None of these needs or reasons is a fad or going any-where anytime soon, so I expect this industry will continue to change the way we live our lives globally for a long time.

Chapter 3

DIRECT SELLING: CAN BE A WAY TO WEALTH

Direct selling has been many people's way to wealth. And I mean people—from eighteen-year-old high school students to senior citizens, from recent college grads to seasoned, currently employed business executives, from world-class athletes to artists, actors, and musicians.

For one thing, consider the tax advantages of the self-employed. As long as you are active in your business and have tangible income, you can receive the tax basis of the self-employed, along with the deductions. For example, being self-employed in a network marketing business lets you deduct car expenses such as repairs, regular maintenance, gas, and oil (your CPA can advise you on what is allowed).

You also can write off the part of your home that you use for business. Many of us have a spare bedroom, part of a basement, or some other space dedicated to our direct-sales business. It's also fine to deduct your travel expenses to and from conventions, meetings, workshops, and regional training seminars. A good CPA can advise you about your options. Another excellent reference is in Robert Kiyosaki's book, "Rich Dad, Poor Dad." Kiyosaki's "cashflow quadrants" provide a visual representation of how people earn income in America today and the value of moving from basic employment to a thriving enterprise, where you reap passive income and where your money works for you.

There are also intangible benefits associated with working in a direct-sales business, such as personal development. We are barraged with bad news on a daily basis. In fact, I generally advise people not to watch the news right before going to sleep. But the world of network marketing is full of great ideas and optimistic people who are trying to accomplish something positive in their lives. It's through direct sales that many of us get our very first exposure to the thoughts and writings of such people as Jim Rohn, Robert Kiyosaki, Dr. Norman Vincent Peale, Dr. Robert Schuller, and others. Even if you don't earn a dime in your first year of direct selling, you will be far ahead in terms of your mind-set, if for no other reason than that exposure to good concepts, which will have changed you for the better.

Joel Broughton

I first met Joel over a decade ago and realized that he had an innovative mind. He was doing marketing on the internet and having success when few others were. That creative thinking has led to great success in MLM. Joel continues to amaze me with how deep a thinker he is and his ability to see how to make things work. He's a very creative person to say the least; here's a recent interview.

I was introduced to MLM in 1999, while I was still in university and 2 months prior to my first children (twins) being born. I was in university full-time, was a Dad of 2 year old twins, worked part-time in the military, and was starting to work and learn about MLM part-time. After university, in 2000, I started working full-time as a military officer (Captain) and was the detachment commander for the recruiting center in our region. I continued to work part-time in MLM and by the end of my military contract in 2004, I had grown my part-time MLM income into a full-time income and started to pursue MLM full-time. I've been full-time in MLM ever since.

The greatest gift that MLM has given to me and my family is CHOICE. It's solely because of MLM that we have had the opportunities to live where we want to live, work when we want to work, and set our own schedules in our lives. I believe that MLM provides the opportunity of choice for everyone. Whether you can build up a full-time income or even just an extra $500 per month, the extra income gives you choices that you normally wouldn't have if you only work a regular 9-5 job. And if you work at it enough, the opportunity to grow your business is endless...which opens up a world of possibilities.

MLM always seems to evolve and change within, but I believe the opportunity only gets better for each generation. As long as we are all willing to grow and adapt with the changes in commerce and technology, the opportunity to grow a substantial income in MLM will always be available for those that want it. When I first started in MLM a whole generation of people laughed at me when I told them that ordering direct from companies and warehouses was the future of shopping. They scoffed and said that shopping malls would never be replaced. We are now living in a time where we see entire malls being closed. The future of distribution is direct to the consumer's home from a company or warehouse...and MLM as an industry is already positioned to capitalize on this monumental shift. The only question left is...are you going to be part of distribution through a MLM or are you just going to watch everyone else's success in the new economy?

Change for the Better

"For things to change, you have to change; for things to get better, you have to get better." I believe that this was a Jim Rohn original, repeated by Larry Thompson and Mark Hughes to many of us network marketers in the early 1980s, and it got us thinking correctly about our futures. If we would make a few changes within ourselves, we could succeed. For me personally, this became a philosophical mantra that I repeated to thousands of people on five continents. Any solid network marketing organization can be the catalyst for a powerful change in people's thinking.

Another intangible benefit of network marketing is the relationships you will forge. In Chapter 1, in talking about the early days, I mentioned some of the folks I worked with, people like Mark Zuckerbrod, Tom Husted, and Larry Thompson. There were others: Suzette Mckay in Saskatchewan, Wally Kralik in Toronto, Foster Owusu in Toronto, Don and Pam Hutchinson, now located in Spain, David and Catharine Haire in Belfast, Dr. Jeffrey Mactavish in London, and others throughout the world who I count as my closest friends today. These folks form my contact capital base for any business in which I engage.

While you may join a direct-sales company initially to earn income, the contact capital you build is where the value lies, and it may last you a lifetime. Through network marketing, you also will cultivate the priceless spirit of entrepreneurial independence. Direct selling gives you the confidence of knowing that you have the skills to prosper anywhere, anytime. Need proof? I have seen several specific groups flourish in direct sales.

Women

Unlike just about any business around, direct sales levels the playing field. In the corporate world, there still may be a disparity between women's and men's salaries. In network marketing, however, if the compensation pays 40 percent retail profit, it doesn't pay a woman 38 percent and a man 40 percent. (By the way, the level playing field also applies to people from different ethnic groups or with alternative lifestyles. Direct sales just may be the fairest form of capitalism there is.)

Women often juggle a tremendous number of responsibilities. If you are a wife and mother, you have household obligations that may limit the time you have to focus on making an income. Or the job you do have may pay you only a minimal hourly wage. Other women struggle to balance family and career, sacrificing time with loved ones to meet critical corporate deadlines. There are also many women out there today raising families on their own. One of the greatest strengths of single moms is the fact that they have given up on the notion that someone else is going to take care of them. Direct sales can be an ideal fit for them—and for any woman who wants financial freedom or wants to make a substantial contribution to the family coffers.

Another great lady who I have worked with is Donna Mann. Donna has a unique perspective.

Network marketing has a way of making people work on themselves, as well being a self-improvement program to use while helping others. I now have the ability to help more people in a more meaningful way than I did when I was working. It has meant I can cash flow my business to suit my needs and the needs of my family. It also means it's an economical way for me to take care of my own health needs and the health needs of many family and a few friends as well. Network marketing has meant a lot to me over the years.

The future of network marketing is very exciting. For the companies that remain ethical, green, science-based and internet savvy, it will be unstoppable. Traditional stores are waning, especially in rural and smaller communities. More and more people shop the internet and use personal shoppers. The younger generation seems to like the personal introduction with the ability to shop and buy from home. They seem more interested in less traditional shopping methods and in health and in the environment as they see it today.

Another great lady we've worked with is Hyacinth Jennings.

Prior to MLM I worked as a lab technician. While I was there, I was introduced to MLM and since then I have found it to be a great opportunity and have not looked back.

Most people, when it comes to speaking in public, are shy and steer clear of it, particularly on stages. I too, was nervous of public speaking due to not being educated in communications. As I obtain new tiers through the business, I had to be on stage speaking to people and overcoming the nervousness I once had by reading books, listening to tapes, and attending seminars. These key events helped me become a success.

In my opinion many are looking for a new opportunity to gain knowledge, have some financial freedom, afford their current payments, save for a vacation, or even retirement. In this day and age, surviving on one income alone isn't enough anymore, therefore having a secondary income benefits not only you but your future.

When you work in an MLM business, you automatically become an independent businessperson, thus being a part of this MLM movement is a chance for anyone to develop their skills. For me personally, my personality traits have been developed due to communicating with people.

In my opinion the future looks promising, as it entails security for me and a promise to those I'm dealing with to better enhance their lives, which gives me a great deal of satisfaction. Also, being in a market that rewards individuals for their effort, doesn't revolve around economic trends, geographical restrictions, or company downsizing, gives a sense of joy that I may be able to reach out to more people.

MLM helps me to grow as a person and feel blessed that I can help those who are looking for new ways to enrich their lives.

I am very grateful for this opportunity from my friend and business partner John to share my thoughts in his book. Thanks to my mentor, Foster, who helped me on my journey of learning and self-development. It is a pleasure working from home and having the freedom to spend time with the grandchildren and helping others building their MLM. I could not have asked for a better opportunity.

I am a mother of three children with seven wonderful grandchildren. MLM is the way into the future. Try it. You will fall in love with it.

Melanie Charron is another amazing lady who lights up a room when she walks in. Recently my wife, Josee, and I had a chance to interview her while in Paris, France.

Where were you prior to your current MLM business?

Before MLM I had a business of head hunting. I invented by mistake a technology that was evaluated at over $5 million dollars 15 years ago. I was young and fresh out of University and I lost everything. In all, I went bankrupt. After that, I was a coordinator for special events with a very large company. I had a great salary.

And now? I am inspiring people by telling them the truth. I was able to achieve my financial freedom 10 months into the MLM business part-time while keeping my full-time job.

For me, the future is clear. Everyone will eventually join a MLM company. Everything costs more than before, and people want to spend more quality time with their family, and they especially need great products to use and sell to earn multiple sources of income, as I have done.

People should join a MLM company to earn extra money, to be able to spend more time with their loved ones, to meet extraordinary people and make true friends (2nd family). It also enables you to help people to become a better version of themselves. My ex-boyfriend was mentally sick! He killed himself along with my 21-month-old son. During this darkest time in my life I realized how many good people there are in the world who supported me. Many were people in my MLM business. That motivated me to keep living and be a beacon of light to others, some of whom are having their own dark times. My MLM business made me see the good in so many other people at a critical time in my life.

Meet Raquel Gojon. My friend Raquel is a lady who has seen the very top of direct selling for over four decades. She is an amazing lady who has the energy of a 30-year-old. She has a smile that attracts people and everyone who meets her is energized by her personality and vision. She is the mother of Susana and Adriana Cazares below—great family.

What did you do before MLM?

I have been in this industry for 41 years. At age 22, we started a grocery store that was successful after 12 years of hard work.

How does your story inspire people?

At the age of 34, I started selling direct as a group leader. I had a great necessity to get ahead for my 5 children; the youngest 1 year and the oldest 12 years old.

I have 42 years in the industry and I am an example of the life of abundance that you can get by helping to improve the lives of other families.

How do you see the future?

The future of the industry depends on the passion we feel, we are the protagonists of this history and we decide if we want to leave a legacy.

Why should people consider MLM as a multiple source of income?

Because it is the industry of the present and the future.

I then met Raquel's daughter, Susana Cazares, while speaking at an event in Mexico. We found that we had many things in common, not the least of which was a passion for athletics and MLM. Here's some of her story.

What did you do before MLM?

Before being in MLM, I had my agency in the music industry; there was good money, but I had no personal life or time for me.

How does your story inspire people?

Because they can see a woman in balance and happy and because they know I'm mama and dad, educating and taking two girls forward.

How do you see the future?

I'm so wrapped up in my company, that the future does not worry me, it gives me confidence and inspires me and my team.

Why should people consider MLM as a multiple source of income?

Belonging to this great business model gives us what we always crave, it allows you to have a real balance, time for me and for all those I love, money and the opportunity to help others.

I first met Adriana Cazares, Raquel's other daughter, five years ago and found a woman passionate about health and physical fitness unlike anyone I have ever known. Whether she's preparing for a marathon, a bike race, or a Pilates class, she is always on the move. She attracts many younger people to her business with an amazing knowledge of health, fitness, and longevity.

What did you do before MLM?

I had an Image Institute, where I taught personality, leadership, health, beauty courses, etc.

How does your story inspire people?

I am a woman who is fulfilling my mission in my life to improve the lives of those around me every day." I live my life with freedom and independence, freedom to enjoy what I love and freedom of time and money; many people around the world want this kind of life.

How do you see the future?

The future in MLM will be extraordinary for everyone who pays the price to be successful in this industry. Everything is written, just learn from the successful people in the industry, learn the basics, do them and duplicate them.

Why should people consider MLM as a multiple source of income?

We have in this industry several ways to earn money. Besides, it is an international and family business.

Rosa Ofelia Pelayo is one of the very top earners in her company. An amazing leader with downline in every country her company has business in. This is a recent interview we did together.

What made you see network marketing as a business and in what year?

The worst financial crisis I have lived through in 2010. I decided at that point to leave nothing to chance and become my own boss.

What has the industry done for you and your family?

The industry of network marketing has allowed me to live the life of true financial freedom; freedom of time for my family and the ability to do what I love to do. I get to spend time with my family, many of which are in my business as well. We get to spend family time and see the world together as we build a family legacy with our business.

How do you see the future?

I see myself developing the current project of building our network like a mission of life where I can truly help the lives of as many human beings as possible to live a better life like we are doing, and blessing many others at the same time.

Rosa has helped numerous people to a better life and has made many people have hope again for the future.

Seniors

Because of economic recessions, senior citizens or those approaching senior status are seeing a major interruption in their retirement planning. That being the case, many have opted to continue earning income via direct sales.

For example, let's say that Bob and Mary are recent retirees who have seen their savings shrink through no fault of their own. They need an extra $2,000 a month to make ends meet, provide for their church tithe, or visit the grandchildren twice a year. Now Bob and Mary have two choices: Put $480,000 in the bank at 5 percent to earn about $2,000 a month in interest or find a direct-sales product or service and earn $2,000 a month between retail sales and bonus money.

Given their age and health status, seniors also can be a terrific match for many of the nutritional products coming out of network marketing these days. And seniors have expanded contact capital. They have seen much in their lifetimes and know many people of various ages. A wise grandmother who finds a promising network business will introduce the opportunity to her children and even her grandchildren. There are loads of senior citizens out there, and with folks living longer these days, seniors are not a group to ignore.

Dr. Barrie White is a man of multiple skills. Versed on the Holy Bible as well as the latest in nutrition, Dr. White is a man of keen interest. Even in his 80's he's a hard guy to keep up with. He is a model of consistency in every respect, from his 50+ year marriage to Ferne, to co-hosting a Wednesday night training call for over 20 years. Consistency produces a great life and Dr. White is all that and more.

When my neighbor presented me with a network marketing opportunity, I could see the big picture within minutes. Sign up, find five who'll sign up and each of them sign up five, and so on. I could be a millionaire within a month. There wasn't any "due diligence". I didn't even know what that term meant.

I didn't ask questions such as is this product needed by most people? Is this a product that customers will consume every month or do you have to find a continuous stream of new customers? Is the compensation plan attractive for me or does it only benefit the owners of the company or those who signed up first? Is the company growing or is it dying? How long has the company been in business since most companies don't even last more than 3 years? Will the product or service be copied and then sold for less? Is the company proceeding in an ethical manner? Does the company have strong leaders?

This first opportunity would have failed on a number of the questions but my work situation in college administration was very toxic and any sign of hope was helpful to my continued sanity. The big, impossible picture won out for the worst of reasons.

Finally, a new company came into my world after I had muddled through several more opportunities. I could recognize the value of the new company since I had learned the hard way (not recommended) of what a worthwhile opportunity looked like. When I finally found my home, I stayed there, successfully, for 23 years.

The earnings have provided a necessary stream of income in my retirement years.

The quality products have been critical to my wife's survival and continued good health. The people who this opportunity attracted became an inner circle of friends and my whole life was enriched.

Network marketing can bring together quality products, financial strength, and great people, A great company provides a nurturing environment, the security of absolute integrity at every level, and relationships that last a lifetime. Network Marketing provides an opportunity for me to make a difference in the lives of many.

Tom Oldershaw is a guy who, despite being in his late 70's, has the look and energy of a man 20 years younger. Tom is driven to help people first and foremost. Here's his story.

Back some 40 years ago I knew of network marketing as a viable and feasible business model.

Today I have chosen a professional career in network marketing, as it offers many positive attributes, including great products, unlimited income, time freedom, personal growth, low start-up costs, along with low risk, and high returns. Network marketing has allowed me to make a commitment of 1 million dollars by 2026 to a worthy cause; helping fund charities involved in providing a hand up to individuals experiencing poverty or homelessness. To accomplish this, an endowment fund has been established. The interest from the capital will allow future funding for the charities of my choice.

The career choice allows me to be able to live a life with a purpose, namely Intentional Living.

The selection of a network marketing career is the best way I know to not only survive, but to thrive in the new economy and I would recommend it for every entrepreneur.

Renald Plamondon is a man of many interests. I had a chance to ask him a few questions about his career recently.

What did you do prior to MLM?

I had a career that started as a 37-year-old federal police officer. After my first years as a patrol officer, I worked for more than 15 years as a major crime investigator. My last 3 years in public affairs was in dealing with the media.

And when you were a youngster?

Previously as a teenager, as a hawker, I had two different newspaper routes. You may ask yourself why two? Because it was two times more pay. Nothing stopped me from achieving my goals then or now.

How did this help shape your thinking later when you joined a MLM company?

In analyzing my career in general, I can today certify that these beginnings as an entrepreneur would influence the rest of my life! I still unknowingly at the time had a plan B. From 15 to 35 years old, for over 20 years, I had my own mobile disco where I had to animate different types of parties, different types of groups of all sizes from 50 to over 3,000 people. In short, a stimulating multiple career that allowed me to develop skills essential to my parallel career in MLM.

How have things turned out from a business you started as a multiple source of income for your family?

A simple investment and time ratio! If you find another way to invest $712 and part time earn me over $2.5 million in 20 years, I do not know any more! I sit on the board of one of the largest private pension funds in North America, we have investments in several other types of funds, in several countries and companies, and never have I seen or analyzed a level of performance as I get and that still gives me time for MLM and will provide to my heirs long term. I never thought a small financial investment and sharing a great product would lead to this, but it has.

I am fortunate to distribute a range of scientifically recognized products that stimulate our immune system. I have been associated with my current company for more than 22 years already.

Our opportunity remains the most modern and efficient, without any financial risk! What's great about MLM is that it provides a low start-up with a chance to make significant money either part time, like it did for me for many years, or even full time, like it does for me now.

What's one of your best MLM memories with your family?

The most beautiful trip, I told my children was going to Walt Disney 2000 (Millennium Celebration) from Montreal to Orlando by car. They probably got tired of hearing my Tony Robbins CD and me telling them that we could afford this type of VIP trip through my income from my MLM business. Yet through hard work we afforded that trip. Tony Robbins played much of that trip and they got the idea that Dad was a believer in self-development. This year, at our condo in Acapulco, surrounded by the whole family this time with our first grandson, I told my children that because our efforts at my MLM business, my spouse Micheline and I were supporters of better health (they are also users of our products and consultants) even for our little grandson! The financial legacy they will all improve on my efforts will be very generous!

And what about the lifestyle, in addition to the important income that has of course and still changes today 22 years later our quality of life, that of my family, my friends and the various social causes that I endorse financially!

Renald is an example of many people who wisely built a business with a solid long-term MLM while having a career elsewhere. Upon retirement from police service he's now able to travel, enjoy his growing family and continue to help other people through his charity work.

Young People

So many young people are looking for more today. Even with an education they wonder how to build a future in the new economy that is driven by the internet. Why not introduce your son or daughter to network marketing now? Bring them to meetings, and the second they are of age, enroll them. Help them today to become exposed to self-development people such as Jim Rohn, Zig Ziglar, and Tom Hopkins, as well as the leaders in your company. In this way, they will have a career in mind instead of a job in mind when they are ready to start their working lives.

Two years ago, I met a young man who has been building a great business in our company. He was 19 at the time and already well on his way to major success. He asked me to speak on a conference call and over 40 people showed up spur of the moment. I knew Gian Carlos Torres was going to do some great things. Here are a couple of questions from a recent interview.

What did you do before network marketing?

Since I am 12 years old, my family & I have been dedicating 70 hours of volunteer work. When it comes to an actual career to maintain myself & my future family economically, I've only done network marketing. I remember being 5 years old & growing up, and imagining, dreaming of me owning an enterprise with me leading thousands of happy employees. Being an entrepreneur, making a HUGE impact worldwide, making tons of money at the same time, was always a goal. Entrepreneurship has always been in my BONES!

How is it working with your mom and family on your business?

Without her experience in network marketing, I would've not been here. We are both pretty independent in a lot of aspects in our business, but pretty dependent in others. She is also better in a lot of aspects, and I am better in others. We complement each other great. The Bible says how plans consulted with others leads to success. She throws a strategy, we speak about it, and vice versa. Even though not working with us now, the support my father has given to us has been tremendous. When he can, he travels with us to all the events. Even my little brother has fun and can quote many of the top leaders and corporate people in our company. We have fun!

As a young person, how do your friends respond when you share what you're doing?

You know, it's interesting. If I am 100% honest, in the beginning, I was so scared to contact them that I didn't contact them, especially through the phone. I actually wrote them a lot of emails because I didn't want to speak to them. With time and improving my skills, some have joined, most haven't. A lot of them found me strange and maybe kind of a "loser" because I decided not to go college immediately after turning 18. In the beginning it affected me, but being connected with mentors like YOU, John, sticking to personal development every day, and going to all the events, made me not care at all. Many of them now have tremendous respect for what I do. Because I worked on my posture and belief that what I was doing was the best career out there, I think some now are believing it. It took time, but was worth it.

How do you see the future?

Whenever I feel down because things aren't going the way I want in my business, I wake up and say: Where else will I get unlimited RESIDUAL income, total time freedom, and the satisfaction that what I am doing is creating a huge impact on others? Network Marketing (NM)! So where else will I go? The key to have a bright future in NM in my opinion is to find a company that is built on rock, not sand, which means find a product that's not good, or great, but extraordinary.

Leaders should care more about you than the actual money and be mission-driven, humble, and interested in developing an entrepreneur brain! Entrepreneurship is tough. You have to develop a certain hunger to succeed and become ridiculously resourceful. You have to be willing to change strategies when things aren't working. You must be willing to go to the events when you are broke. You must have faith that no matter what happens, if others are having success, you certainly will too. Like Eric Worre says: "Network marketing isn't perfect, it's just better. Now, figure it out and go tell the world!"

When you meet Gian Carlos' amazing mom you'll realize where he gets his talent from.

Recently I had an opportunity to ask Mariluz Sanchez Torres a few questions.

What did you do before network marketing?

I come from a family of entrepreneurs. My parents always had successful businesses, one being a record shop in the 70s, a car detailing franchise in the 80s, and a health food store in the 90s. Even as a child I was always involved in the family business. I attended college for two years and married in 1991. After marriage, I worked for an insurance agency for three years, until my first child was born. We had agreed that if we started a family, I would take care of my child. I gave up a good paying job back in the early 90s but preferred to simplify our family expenses to be able to stay home. But life is very expensive, and a child adds to that expense, so I would always look for ways to bring a few extra dollars to the house. I was invited to a network marketing meeting and I fell in love with the concept. I was in love with the idea of being my own boss, making my own hours and determining what I wanted my earnings to be. My family kept growing and I still loved the idea of being able to generate an income without sacrificing what was valuable to me.

After 10 years, circumstances changed. I was diagnosed with stage 3 breast cancer while pregnant. But the blessing of this business is that I was still able to make an earning while doing chemo and while in the hospital for five weeks. But after all was over, my energies were not the same and my emotional state was poor. So, I stopped working for a few years. But network marketing was still my passion. That's when my current company entered my life. It not only helped me regain my health, it also became a family business.

How is it working with your son and family on your business?

Because my children grew up with a networker, you can say that they were networkers in the making. They were part of my achievements. Free cars, trophies, convention recognitions, etc. My daughter is an entrepreneur, but I never knew that my son would join me in this industry. Working with my son has been a game changer. His energy and desire to succeed becomes contagious. In this business or any business, we have to deal with emotional ups and downs. But working together, we've got each other's backs. He is good in the many things that I lack, and I have the experience he is learning from, so we have become a dynamic duo. I wouldn't do it any other way. I learn from his positivism, enthusiasm, and youth.

How do you see the future?

In terms of our financial stability, very positive. I see our family debt-free— financially free. We devote 70 hours each month in volunteer service. Giving is something dear to us. Network marketing can give us that financial stability to continue doing what we love most.

How is it working with your son and seeing his growth both in business and as a son?

Working together with my son is the highlight of my business. Many teenagers are clueless as to what to study or what to do for the future. Gian Carlos was one of those teenagers that had so many ideas in his mind, but still had not decided which path to take. When he gave himself the opportunity to join network marketing, he immediately knew that this was what he loved. He wakes up happy every day looking forward to work each morning. We've always had a close relationship but working this business has strengthened our relationship. He has developed into a very mature young man.

It's funny that usually teenagers don't want to hang out with older folks. Not him! Ha-ha! His friends are probably older than his parents. But this for sure has protected him and continues to help him develop into a very mature man with strong principles.

We've been in the business for almost three years. His professional growth is impressive. I am the one learning from him now.

Raul Tufik is a young man whom I have seen do remarkable things over the last few years in our company, and who continues growing at an amazing pace. Raul is always fun to be around and truly loves people. Here are some of his thoughts on his business.

What first attracted you to MLM?

The possibility of leveraging a team of people with a desire to grow. The concept of residual income impacted me, and I loved how helping others to fulfill their dreams would help me meet mine. In 2016, I understood that if I had a product that covers a biological necessity, people would use it without me needing to be present. That would be the key to success.

How are things working for you?

I place my bank account at the level of my dreams, and try to be an inspiration for many people. I have become a different person, which I never thought possible. I'm a grateful person. I spend more family time and have more tranquility in my life.

How does the future look?

My most powerful dream has always been impacting 100,000 people. In the future, I see the possibility of building something that benefits those 100,000 people and leaves a better world because we were present. Another great dream is to know the space, the planet earth. I already did some research, and this is in the list of dreams to fulfill.

Athletes

If you're an elite athlete, training costs a fortune, with no guarantees of success. Coaching fees, travel expenses, equipment costs, and the like are necessary evils if you have a goal of world or Olympic fame in a given sport. In direct sales, I've worked with many such athletes who have to support themselves while trying to achieve their dreams.

Beyond the financial reasons, aspiring Olympic or college athletes are always looking for an edge that will allow them to train harder, recover quicker, and be in less pain in the process. Direct-sales companies have spawned many nutritional breakthroughs. Athletes are drawn to strong products with legitimate evidence of efficacy. They also form a great testimonial pool for you to build on because everyone wants to use what the high-level speed, strength, or endurance athlete is using.

Fueled by Fame

Network marketing is a great industry for retired pro athletes. The reasons are obvious—lots of notoriety and contacts galore. And where else but direct sales will they find no ceiling to what they can earn? What do those guys do when their huge sports contracts are up? Many of them have chosen network marketing and have lent credibility to our products and our industry.

My buddy, Dennis Schultz, in California, recently entered his first network marketing business.

Although retired from several other ventures, he is building a multiple source of income with a product he enjoys and uses in his training. Dennis has been a world class powerlifter and member of the WABDL powerlifting Hall of Fame, as well as world class competitor in the highland games. The extra money from his networking business offsets some of the cost of travel to events, entry fees, etc. As well it gives him a chance to help people.

Artists, Actors, and Musicians

Creative folks such as aspiring painters, writers, singers, producers, dancers, actors, and directors also can benefit from a direct-sales business. Their training and educational costs can be huge. Most of them end up working as waiters or in other exhausting jobs to support themselves as they launch their careers. Why not introduce them to your network marketing business and show them a way to earn money while working toward their creative goals? I have worked with many talented people, some of whom made it big, whereas others are making a good living in direct sales while enjoying their artistic endeavors as an avocation.

Everyone Benefits

As the last bastion of free enterprise, and full of great tax advantages, direct sales has something to offer just about everyone, whether you're just starting off in business, you just got a pink slip, or you're retired and enthusiastic to add cash to your current cache (especially if the economic downturn did some damage). Here are the key points to keep in mind:

- Direct sales give each of us a fair, level playing field. No matter what your age, gender, ethnic background, or former employment, direct sales has the right opportunity for you.

- This business can be worked around virtually any schedule. Direct sales works for moms who must shuttle kids to practice, people who already work a full-time job, and college students managing hefty class schedules on their way to a degree.

- Direct sales is self-development at its best. Rather than filling your mind with today's latest bad news or dwelling on where the next check is going to come from, this industry will inspire you to reach and grow and develop as a person. I'm talking real confidence and real satisfaction.

- And finally, how about the interesting people who can become part of your permanent contact capital? The direct-sales industry expands your world and your relationships in it. You'll work with some of the finest people you can imagine, and you'll inspire people in your downline to be their finest.

There's no doubt in my mind—network marketing is an open door welcoming all of us to a life of personal and financial greatness. Your opportunity is waiting for you!

Need some proof? Then meet my long-time friend, Arlene Lowy. MLM fell into her life when she was dating a guy who was dabbling in direct sales. Arlene discovered that she liked the products and the idea of MLM. Here's what she has to share.

I've been in MLM for over 40 years, but in the beginning, I had no idea how to work in the business. I started by finding people and information through ads, learning everything I could. Other people were getting great results and earning amazing cash flow in direct sales, and I kept learning. In time, I had my own thriving organization.

As I was building my business, I was also a single mom who had taught children with learning disabilities. Inspired by my efforts to empower these kids to believe in themselves, I applied my teaching skills to my finest student: my son. He became valedictorian of his class and later launched a successful career in the motion picture industry. The thrill of this business for me has always been about wanting more for others' success. Each day I ask myself, "So, whose life will I change today?"

This industry is for everyone, offering a level playing field where your education, race, color, gender, age, and past history do not matter. If you want the best that life has to offer, you need to ask yourself every day, "What am I going to do in these 24 hours to build my business? How will I invest my time?" I did whatever was necessary—even driving through a terrible storm to give my presentation to an empty room of no-shows! And having that mind-set is how I ended up as number 1 in two companies.

Real success in MLM means getting started and hanging with the winners. About 95 percent of the people who join you will treat it like a hobby. Another 4 percent will see it as a business, and that final 1 percent will take MLM to a level where they will do what it takes to have a residual income that lasts forever. Those are the people you enjoy working with the most.

Chapter 4

FAIR DAY'S WORK, FAIR DAY'S PAY

One of the first things you will learn about network marketing is that you need a strong daily method of operation (DMO) to succeed. A DMO is essentially an action plan of specific value-added tasks that you do daily. In network marketing, you don't get paid by the hour; you get paid for results. So how you spend your time really matters. In the early days of building your distributorship, you will need to pay your bills and stay afloat as you develop leadership and sales volume on the back end. (The back end is the over-rides you eventually will receive once you build a downline.) I recommend that you construct your DMO so that you can pay yourself a livable wage.

Let's say that you need to earn at least $100 profit daily to pay your personal overhead. If we assume that your company has a 40 percent retail profit, that the average customer will purchase $100 worth of product, and that your success rate is around 30 percent, you will need to talk to at least ten people each day. Talk to at least 10 people, and on average, three will purchase at least $100 each—so three sales at $100 each = $300 at 40 percent profit = $120 today.

This equation tells you that your DMO needs to get you in front of at least ten people each day. Many of these people simply will want to purchase your retail product and not engage in a new business. Some will have the "I'm from Missouri, show me" attitude and say, "If the products work, then I'm in." Whatever the case, it's your responsibility to sell at least enough product daily to feed yourself and keep the lights on at home.

If your goal was to double your income, you simply would double your efforts. Talk to twenty people to aim for six sales. After doing direct selling for twenty-six years, I know that there are days when it seems like everyone says yes. Sadly, the reverse is also true. But either way, if you keep to this simple formula, it will help you to achieve your target in a big way.

So many business people get involved in MLM after seeing the power of duplication. One such gentleman is Elias Sandoval. I recently had a chance to ask him for a few reasons why he chose our industry.

What did you do before MLM?

Before dedicating myself to the marketing networks, I dedicated all my time to maintaining my own digital marketing business

How does your story inspire people?

The people who have seen me mature in MLM have believed that this does work because of the remarkable change in my personality—emotionally, spiritually and economically. Because of my testimony they have decided to venture into this industry.

How do you see the future?

This industry has a powerful future in the way that people can help others and at the same time benefit themselves.

Why should people consider MLM as a multiple source of income?

This business is as simple as deciding to sell that dish that you love to cook with, getting people who will buy the product monthly, and then recommending others consume.

Stay on the Lookout

An effective DMO begins with a mindset: always be looking out for business opportunities. Let's say that you are working part time with your current network marketing company, and you use a toll road to get you to work. We all know that it's easiest to get a toll counter that allows you to coast through the toll and let the state bill your credit card. I suggest, however, that you pull up to a toll booth with a collector in it instead. That's right, a real, live human being who takes your toll money! I would recommend you have a flyer, a CD, or a DVD to hand to that toll collector, along with your money. The collector really might love his or her job, but chances are that he or she doesn't. Even if he or she does like the job, couldn't he or she benefit from your health and wellness product after breathing car exhaust eight hours a day?

Eventually, this approach becomes a way of life for you. Ask yourself who you give money to each day—the cashier at the grocery store, the bank teller, the dry cleaner, the gas station attendant. There are all sorts of success stories about people who have sponsored folks they see in their daily routine. How about the waiter or waitress? One of the top earners in direct sales joined a network marketing company while he was waiting tables. How would you like to have been his sponsor? You never know who will take the network marketing opportunity and run with it, so always network as you go about your daily activities. That will become your DMO cornerstone.

Let Yourself Be Taught

I refer to this as the "apprentice your way to wealth" approach or the "on the job training (OJT)" concept. The network marketing trade needs to be learned, just like any other trade. I come from a long line of electricians on my father's side, going back at least three generations. Each of those relatives had to spend four years as an apprentice prior to becoming a journeyman. Serving as an apprentice during those lean, early years earns you the right to ultimately earn a much larger salary as a journeyman.

Think about your doctor. Don't you hope and pray that the person who may have the task of saving your life has spent the necessary time developing his or her skill? So why do we get frustrated, even to the point of quitting, when we don't have immediate success? Be patient, and let the learning come to you.

Invest in Seeing Success

Also apply what I like to call the "McDonald's maxim." Imagine that you acquired a McDonald's franchise in your city. After making this major investment, how serious would you be about seeing it succeed? If your restaurant missed the egg delivery because of a snowstorm, you can bet you'd beeline to the local grocery store to buy eggs for your breakfast customers. Why? Because your financial future depends on it. In most cases, you can start a direct-sales business venture for less than $500. But champion network marketing leaders treat their distributorship with the same level of seriousness as if they had invested millions of dollars in a franchise.

Go 10 for 10

An effective DMO incorporates some tried and true tools of the trade, such as the "ten pennies principle." This is an oldie but goodie. It goes like this: every morning, take ten pennies and put them in your left pocket. Every time you have a legitimate conversation with a new prospect about your product, take one penny out and place it in your right pocket. Don't come home until you have all ten pennies in your right pocket. This exercise will become a good habit for you and will help you to develop winning results. I knew a woman who used to fill up her car with her company's weight-loss products early each morning and go out to talk with women about losing weight. She wouldn't let herself come home until her car was empty. That DMO habit ensured that she met her sales goals. And to top it off, the satisfied customers became walking billboards for her product and converted to the distributor ranks after losing weight.

DMOs' To-Do

One of my favorite DMO tools is what I call the "workout routine." I believe that if you are serious about your network marketing business, you should belong to your local gym. As a routine, I still take five CDs, of my current business, with me to the gym and place them in five empty lockers at least three times a week. Of course, the audience at the gym is ideal if you are selling health products, but the DMO habit will get you results with just about any product or opportunity.

You also can try the "three to five DVDs a day" approach. If your network marketing company has a promotional DVD, find a way to lend out five

DVDs a day. Tell the people you loan them to that you have a limited supply, so you'll need them to view it and return it to you within forty-eight hours. This gets the serious people to watch it when they get home that day. And always remember that the fortune is in the follow-up. You need to consistently circle back to those folks to get results.

Everything you do in your DMO should be designed to get you to direct-sales business's primary sales vehicle—the meeting. I believe that your meetings should last thirty minutes at most. We were all raised on half-hour-long TV shows, padded with ten to twelve minutes' worth of commercials. Chances are that the only key points that your prospect will remember from your meeting are product results and your income testimonials.

Meeting Formats

There are several formats for network marketing meetings. Here are the ones used most by people in our industry:

- Group meetings in hotels, coffee shops, church halls, etc. allow you to have contact with as many people as possible from your downline, as well as their current prospects.

- Two-on-one meetings involve you and a new member of your downline going out and seeing his or her first three prospects. You do the talking and let this serve as on-the-job training for your new recruits. The new recruit's job is simply to make the introduction.

- Home meetings are popular because people can dress casually and enjoy the comfort of a home environment. Home meetings tend to be highly effective. Here are a few reasons why: People generally feel financially pressured at hotel events or office meetings. When they come to your home, though, they can concentrate on the meeting and metabolize the details of the product and opportunity better. Another reason the home meeting works well is the zero-cost factor. The prospects can see themselves holding meetings in their own homes because the only cost is perhaps some coffee or bottled water. This creates a process that is easy to duplicate.

- One-on-one meetings involve just you and your prospect. It's critical to use your best visual tools in a one-on-one format. Results sell. If you have a product that is visual, such as one for weight loss, use the best before and after pictures with your prospect. This also works on the business side with potential distributors. Use stories from your company magazine of people who have purchased new cars, homes, and more with their business earnings. Most people are visual, so show results of product use and earnings.

- Telephone/internet-based meetings involve using one or more technologies to communicate a message about your business. Examples of this are conference calls and webinars—both very effective for communicating with potential customers or recruits who live in another state or another country.

Today many of us use technology such as Facebook groups, Instagram, and a newer technology called Zoom to get our message out. Using these platforms, we can truly work from home and see our prospects as well as we could if we were in the same room.

These technologies are also very effective when it comes to working with and leading your downlines. You want to establish monthly organizational meetings with your downline team to cover new business items such as upcoming meetings in your area, the company's monthly incentives, or any special advertising being done as a group. Also use these monthly organizational meetings to recognize and celebrate new rank advancements by your leads. Your monthly team meetings are most effective if scheduled around the first of each month.

Carry the Key Messages

Whatever the venue, or meeting format, there are five key messages that you must impart to be effective in your direct-sales meetings. I recommend that you cover the following material and use the suggested time limits to keep your meeting around the thirty-minute mark.

Your company and who runs it (five to seven minutes): Give some brief information about your CEO, key staff members, and who manages sales.

Your anchor product (five to ten minutes): Explain what sells and creates predictable income. For example, if you have a product with patents, clinical trials, or other black-and-white science, you need to make that information available. If your product has testimonials from the medical community, use those as well—but don't get too technical. Leave the white lab coat at home! Remember, you are also trying to recruit people into marketing your product or service. If they think that they need an Ivy League education to understand the product, they may buy as a customer but not see themselves marketing it comfortably.

If you are not marketing nutrition or health-related products, then who supports your product? Is there a financial group, such as a major investment group, that is backing your company (assuming that your company is public)? If not, are there articles from magazines or on the internet about your company? If so, use them. Remember: Documentation beats conversation. The more proof positive the presentation is about your product, service, or business model, the better.

Your product's results (ten to fifteen minutes): As stated earlier, before and after stories and/or photos are extremely effective. Remember, results sell, and sell, and sell.

The compensation plan (ten to fifteen minutes): Offer a short, simple explanation of the retail, wholesale, overrides, and monthly incentive aspects of the compensation plan.

Your story (five to ten minutes): Tell your prospects how long you've been with the company, what product you market, and your income results. Learn to package your story. How long have you been using your product or marketing your product or service? What results have you had? You can start with, "My name is John, and I lost fifty-five pounds in eight months using XYZ, and I also earned $30,000 marketing this product part time" or "My name is Mary, and I purchased ABC service and have saved $3,000 so far, as well as earned $2,000 part time sharing the business with others."

Also cite the product and income results of other leaders in your company. I like to use at least three stories of other high producers to show that people besides me are having product and business results. Once again, documentation beats conversation, and results sell.

Lead by Doing

Remember, champion direct-sales distributors lead by example. Since you are the leader of your downline, your people will do what you do, not what you tell them to do. So, if your company has a trip incentive, make sure you qualify for it. Show your people that you are willing to do what you want them to do. Achieve and lead from the front of the pack.

As one of the "big guys" in my company, I am always bringing on new people. After a recent conference call, a woman in my business sent me an e-mail congratulating me for bringing in a savvy new person who also had been on the call. I e-mailed her back saying, "Lori, there are many equally strong people out there looking for an opportunity. So, thanks, but let's go get you a good new recruit too." Within a week, she had sponsored a new, experienced couple who were ready to move in a big way with our enterprise.

If you treat your direct-sales business as a hobby, you will get hobby income at best. Instead, create a strong DMO, use meetings to your best advantage, commit to learning from your upline and corporate leadership, and be willing to try new approaches to advance your personal and group momentum.

Chapter 5

Your Opportunities with Direct Selling

Since starting my first direct-sales business in 1983, I've seen this industry evolve and change in powerful ways. I have to say that nothing has made a stronger impact on the business than the technological advances we now take for granted.

We've gone from relying on face-to-face presentations and phone conversations to using cell phones, laptops, and personal digital assistants (PDAs) that let us talk to, text, email, or instant message a person in our downline from wherever we are. Whether a businessperson is checking out your website from his or her computer down the block or joining your monthly webinar, with hundreds of other people from all over the world, the internet has enabled a potential customer or distributor to learn about you and your business at any time. Other technologies have made it possible to upload customer information and download custom-tailored solutions in a matter of seconds. The potential reach of your business is now on a global scale, and information exchange takes place in real time.

No doubt about it, technology now provides reliable and dynamic tools for doing business. But, the use of technology is also where I see people screw up. It is possible to rely too much on technology and lose the most important aspect of our business—the human touch. According to many internet experts, a businessperson reads only about 10 percent of the email he or she receives. Those savvy salespeople you'd like to have on your team are often skimming through hundreds of messages a day, and it's too easy for them to delete yours.

Face-to-face communication will always matter. It's one of those points of difference about the network marketing business that you'll read about in a later chapter. Looking back to when I started in direct sales, I went to people's houses and held meetings with distributors in my home. Jump ahead close to thirty years, and I still go to peoples' houses. Meetings, public business receptions, and seminars still create that special atmosphere for engaging potential customers and distributors. And that's your primary goal—to create an environment where you and your distributors can link arms to build a successful business together.

Yes, you'll use your laptop to do such things as run CDs, DVDs, and PowerPoint presentations. You'll need a good website, and you'll want to take advantage of internet tools to promote your business. Webinars will continue to be an amazing way to meet with your downline, especially when your distributors are spread out across the country or around the world. At the end of the day though, the purpose of technological tools is always to serve your people and to foster person-to-person business relationships. Network marketing will always be about people development, and face-to-face contact is hard to beat.

Another constant of the direct-sales business is the importance of a targeted message. The message has to fit the person with whom you are communicating—whether the conversation is one-on-one over coffee, or over a long-distance call by web phone. What you say needs to be timely and relevant for that person, where he or she is in his or her life right now. This kind of customizing is tough to package in an email blast. It's even more challenging when you realize that your business is no longer about chatting up a distributor opportunity with your neighbor or recruiting your family members. Technology has opened up much of the modern world to the expansion of your business—you can't even assume that your next customer or distributor will speak the same language.

Despite the constant barrage of new technologies I have witnessed over the past twenty-five years in network marketing, I have to say that, without question, this business has been and always will be about people serving and helping people. If this has you charged up, get ready to find the right opportunity for you. Whether you are a retired businessperson entering the world of network marketing for the first time or someone looking to expand into a new direct-sales business, there are certain criteria to consider for your ultimate success.

Find the Right Fit

First, if you don't believe in the product or service, why go there? If there's no attraction or personal relevance, why would you want to go there? While it's not always an exact science, you must recognize some kind of fit between you, your lifestyle, your experience, and the product or service you are representing. It needs to be something you'd use or recommend easily, or something about the business must get your heart pumping.

When you are considering a first business or an add-on business, you need to start with whether the offering matches up with who you are, what you do, what you care about, and the contacts you have in your Rolodex. For example, if you're in the healthcare field, distribution of health-related products is a natural fit for you. You know the science, and you probably have a sizable contact list already. Ask yourself: Do the products fit who I am and/or what I am already selling?

My litmus test for a new product or service is what I call my "chicken list." There are certain people who most of us don't feel comfortable talking to about our lives or our business. The list might include your doctor, your accountant, your lawyer, or even your minister. It could include some mega-successful business name from another industry. If you met Bill Gates on an elevator, would you feel comfortable telling him what product you are selling? When you're at a party with people you don't know, can you say, "I'm in the X business" with enthusiasm? In other words, can you talk about your product or service to your "chicken list" without feeling embarrassed? If so, it's probably a good fit.

Sometimes, though, your faith in the business wins out in the "chicken list" test. One of my earlier businesses involved diet cookies. There I was, a successful business guy who also was a recognized athlete and martial artist, talking up these amazing cookies. People on my "chicken list" sort of smirked and chuckled, but I laughed all the way to the bank. The diet cookies were an exceptional product, and they had good business minds, good science, and good marketing behind them. I believed in that business, and my belief trumped the "chicken list" skeptics.

Joining or expanding a business also means taking the time to examine the business model behind the brand. This due diligence includes getting a clear picture of the current state of the business, the marketing tools you'll have to work with, the training program, the company leadership, and the compensation plan.

New May not Be Better

It can be tempting to join a new startup company, especially if the leadership includes people with a strong track record in another industry. Even if the CEO has been featured in Fortune Magazine or has taken another direct-sales organization to the top, it will take him or her time to really know how a new business works, how to attract the right people, and how well a new product or service is received by consumers.

Unfortunately, most startups in our business fail or stumble around in the beginning years while all the bugs are worked out. Give a new business two to three years before jumping on board. This waiting period gives the company a chance to smooth out the edges, survive review by the Federal Trade Commission and other regulatory bodies, and soften the market. It also takes two to three years for the real movers and shakers to join the team. They've been out there. They've been watching and waiting for the dust to settle—and so should you.

Check the Tool Belt

When it comes to promoting your business, some companies offer great science behind the products but fall short on the marketing side. Others market like champions, but the science is a little hazy. Find the business with the right balance. Marketing tools must begin with a branded, easy-to-navigate website that clearly highlights the benefits of the product and the business. A good internet strategy is also a must, especially if you plan to make use of the myriad tools available online, such as e-newsletters, e-zines (online magazines), blogs, social networking sites such as Facebook, newer technologies such as Twitter, webinars, or YouTube to present your product or business.

As for tangible offline marketing tools, the company should have a variety of eye-catching and effective pamphlets and other print materials for you to buy at an affordable price and use confidently with your new customers or distributors. And keep in mind that no distributor should be looking to make a profit on the sales of sales tools. A small markup is fine. Distributors who sell tools to their downline with forty or fifty cent per piece markups are doing their business and their people a disservice.

Get Good Training

A business that is worth joining is one that has a strong core philosophy about training. It's simple associative math: The people downline will only be as good as the upline distributors who are teaching them. Your upline people are your coaches and mentors, and they should want you to have a full, clear understanding of the company and its products or services. They need to be accessible and ready to answer your questions and to guide you when it comes to improving your skills.

You want to know how training is managed and maintained in the business, and how best practices are shared. Will you be joining in weekly conference calls with your upline person? Are there regular seminars? If it looks like you're going to be handed a startup kit and then left to fend for yourself, walk away.

Strong upline people will want to help you build your business, but they won't do the work for you. Chinese philosopher Lao Tzu said, "Give a man a fish and you feed him for a day. Teach him how to fish and you feed him for a lifetime." Strong leaders will help you leverage your contact capital and coach you in presenting the opportunity—but you'll be the one doing the work.

In Chapter 1, I mentioned how former President Ronald Reagan's commencement speech made an impact on my life. He talked about finding someone who takes an interest in teaching you—a mentor. The people who will train you are supposed to be mentors and messengers of action. No one should train just to hear the sound of his or her own voice. If the person training you sees it as an opportunity to hold court instead of teaching you and motivating you to action, find a new mentor.

On the flip side, if you are in the trainer role, you are responsible for helping your people to hone their skills. This means that you need to meet them where they are in their lives. There will be downline people who have been part-time for eons, only to lose their job and need to do their direct-sales business full time. In a down economy, you'll also meet people who have enjoyed immense professional success and have been handed a pink slip. These folks may know nothing about direct sales or may be highly skeptical.

My own career success is mainly from knowing how to choose the right opportunity for my business mix, and how to find the right people to join my team. I speak regularly with smart, established businesspeople who have no network marketing background. Seasoned, successful sales executives in fields such as real estate, finance, consumer products, or insurance already know how to put people first and that true success relies on acquired skill, hard work, persistence, and strong leadership. They'll need a mentor, someone willing to teach them, and I know how to take on that role.

Your True Riches

Money and wealth are wonderful but getting the skills you need is golden and worth more than any amount of cash in the bank. The true proof of great training is that if you were dropped anywhere in the world, you could succeed because of the skills you've acquired.

I'm an educator, and this means that I'm dedicated to training my downline people so that they understand the business and get the skills they need. I also tell them, "Go out there and get your nose bloodied." Sometimes you're going to fail or make a mistake. If you're like most of us, someone you know is going to tell you to go out and get a "real job." My advice is always: "Just pick yourself up and try again. You've got the skills, and success means that you keep getting up when somebody or something knocks you down."

Who's on Top?

Ideally, your mentor will be directly upline from you, the person who encouraged you to start your own network marketing business. Still, if you want to talk to the person on top making crazy money every month, a good business should be able to make that happen. The truth is that you don't have to be sponsored directly by the top-level people, but you should never be denied access to them.

You might not be able to just walk into the CEO's office, but if you have a question or an idea to share, a top person should be available to you by phone or email (as long as the subject is relevant). You want to have access to the people who make it all happen, and they should want to listen and share the wealth of their experience. If you sense that there's a force field denying you access to the top players in the company, it's probably time to look for a better opportunity.

This is an altruistic business, so why would anyone want to hold downline people back? I tell my distributors that it's not about you and your ego. If you want to be more successful, make your downline people more successful. The founders and leaders of top network marketing companies preach this philosophy. Bottom line: Network marketing works from the bottom up.

My friend, Karen Ford, is one of those people who knows what it takes to be successful in MLM and who unfailingly does what is necessary to rise to the top, despite those curveballs that life can throw at us. Here she shares from her own experience:

"When I met John in 1994, I was a single mom making some good money in direct sales, but John saw more in me than I could see in myself. He offered to take me under his wing, asking me if I would do what he said to be successful. Of course, I said yes.

John's first order of business that day was to ask me to commit to the 10 Penny Rule: Contact 10 new people per day, every day. That first day, my nerves got to me, and I didn't go through my 10 pennies. But the next day John pushed me to get past my fears, and after adding the unused pennies from the day before, I made the calls—all 15 of them. Just 120 days later, I broke into a six-figure income.

John once told me, "You are an eagle, Karen, not a buzzard. You will fly with the eagles." That encouragement mattered when my first company ended my distributorship, and I found myself back at the beginning. I connected with John, found a new company, and started duplicating the process that had worked the first time, starting with the 10 Penny Rule. After seven months, I am now my new company's fastest growing distributorship.

At a recent convention where I spoke, my give-away to each attendee was a little bag with 10 pennies in it. You see, you may be able to take away my paycheck, but no one can take away the skills that have brought me success."

Making Money

Of course, once you see that a company offers products or services that consumers want at prices that they want to pay, you'll need to make sure that there's a good, clear compensation plan in place. If you don't get how the plan works, you can be sure that your prospects will find it confusing, too. In fact, you need to be able to explain your compensation plan to prospects in a few sentences. Here are some examples:

- Let's say that the business involves a retail profit, where the plan pays you 30 percent. If you sell $100 worth of products and services at 30 percent, then your profit is $30. The product or service price is what it is, and there are no markup factors to consider.

- If the compensation plan is based on wholesale, make sure that the wholesale price is low enough to handle a reasonable retail markup. If wholesale cost is too close to what people see as the anticipated retail price, there's no room for a markup—and that can feel like starting out behind the eight ball. Your profit with a wholesale plan might look like this: A new person you've recruited might get a 10 percent discount on what he or she sells, whereas you, as his or her upline person, get 30 percent. You're paid on the difference in percentages, so if the difference is 20 percent, $100 worth of products sold by your downline person nets you $20.

- Plans with overrides are simple to understand and explain. You recruit Mary, and she sells $2,000 worth of product. If your override is 5 percent of what she sells, you make $100.

I've learned that it's best to use round numbers when explaining my compensation plan to a prospect. People need to be motivated by the plan, but the truth is that most people don't fully understand it until they get their first check.

What if a business already has a lot of reach (market saturation) or has been around for decades? Is there still real opportunity for you? The answer is probably. Remember: it's a global market out there, and your goal is not to play it safe by recruiting your best friend or your hair stylist—although you might target your stylist as a prospect if you're selling hair products.

There are about 160 countries around the world open for business and ready to embrace new products, services, and opportunities. New technologies can bring your message right into homes in Australia or Mexico. If you have distributors in, say, France or Japan, you'll train and support them, and they, in turn, will provide the cultural understanding and personal one-on-one touch to grow the business.

Finding Multiple Sources of income

With the economy in its current state of turmoil, offering a business owner multiple sources of income within the walls of his or her current business is a blessing. You will be rewarded for providing a good opportunity at a bad time.

Everywhere you look, you see people who have discovered that network marketing is the ideal opportunity for enhancing the products or services they already offer. Frankly, I've got more stories about those people than I can fit in this book. A perfect example is Dr. Jeffrey MacTavish:

Dr. Jeffrey, as we call him, has built a very successful life in the medical world in a beautiful oceanfront town in the UK. Yet he is always looking for ways to challenge himself. So, he entered a networking company and became a leader in his part of the world. He has an interest in health, so he markets a health product. He has found a way to use both his credibility and creativity to create a great MSI.

The Soul of Business

Small-business entrepreneurs are the soul of network marketing, especially here in the United States.

They can adapt, sustain, and build their teams even during the harshest of economic climates. I've seen hundreds, if not thousands, of ordinary people who have taken a hit like a job loss pull themselves up by the bootstraps, and enter the world of direct sales.

Take Wally Kralik from Ontario, Canada. Wally was the largest independent retailer in Ontario for many years. Owing to the economic downturn, he found himself near fifty and near broke. Rather than wallow in self-pity, he sought out his first network marketing business. He learned the basics, did well, and today in his second venture earns a small fortune annually. Now in his 70's Wally has the time and financial resources to enjoy his grandchildren as they grow up. The ballgames and other activities he missed with his own kids he now gets to have a second chance at, while continuing to earn a great income, as well as creating a legacy for his family.

Dr. Vicky Dominguez was looking for a way to stay at home and use her skills to help people. She found a direct-sales product that she understood and could market, not only in her new nation of Canada, but also in her prior home in the Philippines.

These are a few of the championship distributors I know. There are many more around the world who have found a better way. While direct selling is not easy, once you acquire the skills, they are yours for life. In some cases, those life skills create extreme wealth. In just about all cases, they help people to realize a better quality of life if the proper energy and commitment are instilled and maintained.

For the most part, success is a choice. Tell yourself today and every day that you choose to win, to be a champion. The great NBA coach, Pat Riley, was known to tell his Lakers teams, "The fans are here, you're here—we might as well win." My message to you is that your network marketing opportunity is here, you're here—so get out there and win!

Chapter 6

MARKETING YOUR POINTS OF DIFFERENCE

In today's world of direct sales and network marketing, consumers are faced with companies and product offerings that appear very much the same and may in fact be the same. How do you establish your company and what do you offer that is different, unique, or better? From the perspective of the customer—why should I join your company or purchase your product instead of considering other options?

The critical elements that set you, your product, and your company apart from all the rest are your points of difference. These points of difference are what make you stand out from the crowd, giving your prospect a compelling reason to listen to your story, invest time building your business, or choose to buy your product or service.

It Starts with You

To identify and understand your points of difference, you must start with the most important part of your business—you.

What is your point of difference? What makes you unique as a sponsor or a sales representative of your product line? Think about it: The first thing you have to sell is yourself. If your prospect doesn't resonate with the essence of who you are as a person and business professional, he or she certainly won't choose to buy your product or join your business. You've probably met certain salespeople and walked away saying to yourself, "I would never buy from that person." And yet someone else across the room may have a certain something that could inspire you to jump onboard or pull out your checkbook in a New York minute.

Each of us is unique. We all have different backgrounds, accomplishments, and experiences. Even those of us who are engaged in the same profession go about it differently. You need to identify what's unique and special about you—your point of difference—and to do that, you need to step back and do a serious self-appraisal.

A word of advice: Self-appraisal can be a tricky business, and quite often we are unaware of the qualities in ourselves that others may find obvious. We may even disagree with what others see as our qualities. In fact, if you asked your close friends to fill out a questionnaire about your uniqueness, you'd probably be startled by some of the comments.

Don't be surprised if, during this process of self-appraisal, you find some things that are unique, but not necessarily in a good way. Some aspects of who you are or how you do business will need adjusting, and identifying those aspects is the first step.

When it comes to identifying some of your unique qualities, I recommend that you start by throwing away all your own perceptions about who you think you are and how you may come across to others. I've discovered that your perceptions are most likely invalid anyway. Instead, grab a pen and a notebook, and get ready to zero in on your unique points of difference.

It's About Your Personal Attributes

What is it that people want to know about you? This question is powerful for identifying what draws people to you and makes them interested in your business. Maybe you're poised, always dressing professionally and looking like a successful businessperson. Perhaps you have an outgoing, enthusiastic, can-do attitude that people notice immediately. Or maybe you're more laid back and able to make a new person feel comfortable and at ease within minutes. What is your natural appeal when someone approaches you? Is there anything about your personal presentation that could use some improvement?

A prospect will also want to know your professional history, and that can range from your being new to the business, to years of experience in the direct-sales industry, to decades of success in another industry. New people will want to know your business goals for the future and how you plan to accomplish them. A potential distributor will want to know what it's like to have you for a sponsor. All this means that you need to know your specific qualities, what motivates you, what professional experience you have to offer, and what skills you can share.

There is an adage about our industry that says, "Would you want to sponsor you?" What this means is this—Do you have the right attitude, the right posture? Are you a student of the game, meaning do you know your product or service well, and do you comprehend how the pay plan works? Also, do you understand the intangibles of the business well enough to make them clear to others. Do you know when to use the right tools in different circumstances or markets?

Next, how would you briefly chronicle your background experience? Why did you join your current business, and how committed are you? Take some time in your notebook to outline your success stories. If you have a degree in business, that's a plus. If you never went to college, jot down the wins you've accomplished in the jobs you've had. Remember, direct sales is everyone's way to wealth.

Whether you've run a Fortune 500 company, managed retail salespeople, or taught second graders, you have special skills and success stories that relate to your business and that highlight your attributes. Identify any accomplishments that you've garnered in your business and know what you plan to accomplish soon.

Another area to assess is your training skills. What's it like to be trained by you? Do you have an organized plan to help a recruit get started? These questions are critical because new people need to know that you'll be there for them and how you will support them—and they deserve realistic expectations of what your support looks like. Are you successful at doing three-way calls once a month, or is your strength more about holding weekly conference calls with a large group? Perhaps you get best results with smaller weekly face-to-face meetings in your home. Know what works for you and what you have to offer your prospects.

You also want to assess your presentation skills. They say that public speaking is one of many people's greatest fears. That being the case, when I began my career, I was too shy to get in front of the room. However, one of my mentors, Tom Hopkins, gave me a little advice on the back of a business card. Tom Hopkins wrote, "Do what you fear most." Over the next few presentations, I would look at the message written on that card by one of, if not the, greatest salesman in the world and tell myself, "I can't let

Tom down." Because I transformed my fear of rejection to the desire not to let down someone, whom I greatly respected, I spoke with clarity (even though I was scared to death).

Many times, today, when I bring new people to the front of the room to speak or to be recognized, as I greet them I whisper in their ear that they should pretend the audience is naked. Now that may sound funny, but it works. Once again, it takes the power away from fear. At a recent meeting in Toronto, a young lady from Bulgaria came to the front to be recognized for achieving a new rank in our company. Of course, I whispered in her ear that the members of the audience were all naked. She went from fear to being real and herself, and the audience responded with great applause for both the woman and her story.

Finally, how good are you at helping others to become successful? If you are committed to the success of your team, but continue to see falloff six months after new distributors sign up, that's likely a sign that the training and support you provide are not up to par. Maybe your recruitment efforts aren't drawing the right kind of people, and you need to get better at assessing the potential of your prospects. Helping your people to be successful is about providing good customer service on the internal side of the business, and relates to how your customers feel about how you do business. If you go out of your way to provide great customer service to your distributors and your customers, you have a point of differentiation worth its weight in gold.

Capitalizing on Your Unique Attributes

After you've written down your assessment answers, take a few minutes to underline what you see as your unique qualities, the attributes you have that stand out. You are looking for "hooks" that you can use to capitalize on for all your unique qualities. How can these qualities become a point of difference for you, allowing you to better promote yourself and your business? An important point to remember as you are identifying your key qualities: For the most part, your prospects will only care about qualities that will benefit them! Using that filter, examine what points of difference empower you and your business and what areas could use some improvement.

Let's say that you've got a track record for setting goals and accomplishing them and that some of your strong suits include exceptional interpersonal communication skills and people management. Your points of difference probably pivot around your key quality as a natural leader. Whatever goals you set, your team will take the baton from you and race on to success.

Maybe you're a natural at presenting your sales pitch and attracting new members to your business team—but you've been frustrated at the slow results shown by many of your new recruits. Your positive points of difference obviously include your innate charisma and enthusiasm—you can win over anybody—but maybe your training and coaching skills need some improvement. Remember, self-examination can uncover some weaknesses that need your attention, and that spells opportunity.

Many years ago, in the United Kingdom, I met a man who had been very successful in the corporate sales world. Peter had done well selling everything from computers to insurance. As he became involved in direct selling, he had no trouble selling the product. However, his downline group never really grew exponentially, despite the good growth of other groups with far fewer sales skills.

One day he asked if he could buy me dinner and discuss his frustrations. I agreed, and over a couple nice steaks, we discussed his approach with his people. Peter was extremely polished, a great dresser, and he was always ready to work, to say the least. However, I pointed out to him that he was too put together, always trying to impress his prospects with how smart he was. Perhaps it would help if he could stumble over a few words the next time he spoke. Perhaps he also could have a few of his current distributors speak during the meeting as well—let them feel like they were part of the process. I even suggested that he dress down a bit. (And none of this was what he wanted to hear.)

However, I also pointed out to Peter that his business was a team effort and that the business would never grow if he didn't allow for the growth of some of his less sophisticated distributors. Peter told me, "I'll try it your way." My response to that was to reinforce that it was not my way and that the principle had been tested and proven correct by many who came before me. He began moving aside in the process of building his team's success, allowing others to participate more fully. He also relaxed and became a little less "all about sales." Peter's business started to grow, and he became one of the stars in his company.

Attracting the Right People

When building a successful network marketing business, the kind of person you are correlates directly with the kind of people you want to attract. Are you using the laws of attraction to attract the right kind of people with whom you want to work? Are you regularly meeting people who are worth working with and willing to be coached? If not, go back and read one of the great books on the law of attraction. Suggested readings are included in the resource section of Chapter 10. Nobody wants to work with or even be around negative people, and you certainly don't want to be in business with them. If you have the "million-dollar attitude," the right people and the income eventually will come your way.

It's About Your Company

Picture this scenario: Susan Jones, CEO of your company, is an extraordinarily sharp woman who is not only formally educated in management but also the notably successful president of XYZ Company before taking over as CEO of your company. Susan knows business. She knows the industry, and most importantly, she has a proven track record of guiding a company down the road to success.

If this vignette describes your company and your CEO, do you know what that would mean for you? How could you lose? You attracted and hired a savvy business maven to run your company and keep it on the success track. Think about what a key point of difference it would be, being able to talk with a new prospect about your company's stellar leadership team and how that professional power is behind every person who works for you!

Get ready to write in your notebook again, answering these very important questions about your company:

- Who is your CEO or president? It is essential that you know the qualifications of the person who runs your company and that he or she has a background that you can trust. Begin with knowing where he or she attended college and if your president or CEO has field experience or a thorough understanding of the direct-sales industry.

- What's the vision for your company, and what's the plan to get there? A good company leader will always have a vision of the future and a roadmap for how to make the company successful. Executing the vision means having the right people in place to benefit your business. Looking at your entire team, what team members does your company have in place, and what makes each one a benefit to your prospects? How many of your company executives have significant network marketing, direct-sales, and/or management backgrounds?

Just as you did with your own points of difference and finding those quality "hooks" about you, identify what makes your company unique and special—and then share it with your prospects. One new company I know has hired twenty-three former executives of a major company that specialized in its area. Now that's smart! That's a point of difference that every distributor can capitalize on when giving a presentation to a new prospect. It builds confidence in your prospect's mind that your company has a solid foundation for field support. With that kind of experience and power behind your company, any wise, prosperity-minded person will see all the signs of potential success.

It's Always About Your Product

The product or product line is the foundation of any successful company. Whether your prospect is to become a customer or a distributor, he or she needs to know what it is that you are marketing, and why anyone should buy it. Here is an absolute rule of thumb about products:

- Customers remain customers only to the degree that they have confidence in the products you are selling. Good distributors remain good distributors only if they are truly sold on the value your product.

For Nutrition and Weight-Loss Products

For nutrition products, you want to know and understand the science that supports your flagship product and who says so besides you. What studies, doctors, universities, hospitals, etc. have examined and reviewed your product? What makes it different or better or more effective than the competition? And most importantly, why should I buy it? What benefit will I receive?

Weight-loss products are one product where testimonials really work because you can see the results. Interestingly, although you will want to know the science behind the product, medical studies won't hold as much credibility as the testimony of someone who has gotten great results. These people are walking commercials for your product!

Imagine yourself at a networking event, talking to a new prospect. "Sally, let me tell you what [name of your product] has done for me," you say. "I've been using the super-duper weight-loss program for forty-five days, and I've lost twenty-two pounds. I feel better than I have in years. And my wife started a few weeks after me, and she's lost fourteen pounds and three dress sizes so far!" Your product is probably as good as sold in about a minute—especially if you make it a habit to have a before picture with you for comparison.

If you don't yet have a personal experience or you don't need to lose weight, don't worry—you'll have dozens of testimonials that you can borrow from satisfied customers or other distributors. That's the value of meetings and gatherings. I mentioned carrying a before picture of yourself if you are your own walking testimonial. For weight-loss products, get in the habit of obtaining before and after photos of people for whom the product has worked. And learn the stories of the people in the photos, collecting anecdotes such as how long it took to lose weight and how much weight they lost.

Remember, for nutrition and weight-loss products, results sell. People are busy, and twenty-four hours after they meet you, your prospects will barely remember your name or the name of your company. However, they will remember results, and that should motivate them to buy, if they haven't already done so.

For Other Products

What if you're selling a physical product such as clothing, jewelry, or candles, or an intangible item such as legal memberships, insurance, or telecommunications? Once again, you need to identify the features and benefits that make your product special and different. One of the companies with which I consult has a beautiful line of women's clothing. However, the same type of clothing can be found at most high-end retailers. Here are some of the points of difference on which the direct-sales company capitalizes:

- The high-end retailer won't come to your home or office and let you try on a piece of clothing when and where it is convenient for you—but this company will.

- A high-end retailer also won't give you a discount on additional sales. This company? It's common practice for the distributor. How about earning discounts?

- If you tell your friend about a cool boutique, the store owner will rarely, if ever, reward you for the referral. You earn discounts with this company every time you refer a new customer.

Get the idea here? Service sells big time, especially for busy female executives, working moms, or even stay-at-home moms with children.

Speaking of women in the direct-sales business, one company with which I consult actively communicates how it empowers women financially. This is a powerful point of difference! Others market how their services make a positive impact on groups of people that usually are deprived of services that the wealthy in society can easily afford. At the most basic, even a simple discount price might be your point of difference.

Let's take a detour and look at how some companies outside the direct-sales world approach their point of difference compared with their competitors. A major American insurance company is an excellent first example. The company offers ultracompetitive rates and will be happy to provide rates for you immediately. The company also stores your quote information, just in case you are not ready to buy today, or your other coverage hasn't expired yet. Want to call back in three months? "No problem, Mr. Jones or Ms. Smith. We've got your information right on file!"

Another example is a leader in the banking industry. This well-known company decided to have its banks open seven days a week in several key U.S. markets. Do you remember the term bankers' hours, which used to mean that timeslot between 9:00 a.m. and 3:00 p.m., when most of the population was busy working? Well, these folks are open most days until 7:00 p.m. and even on Sunday afternoons. They've figured out that in a highly competitive business such as banking, they should stress their point of difference: "We are open when you aren't working!" Imagine that—and it only took about 150 years for the banking industry to figure out what works best for the customer.

As I've said before, great service is always a valuable point of difference. You can see that unique quality in action when you shop at one of the most successful department store chains in existence. This retail business has been famous for years for its superb customer service, its friendly staff, and its "ask no questions" return policy. Great service in a hassle-free environment is the point of difference that keeps this company's customers flocking to its stores—both brick and mortar and online—time and time again. If it works for this company, is this a point of difference that you can adapt and make beneficial for your business?

A final example is the famous retail coffee shop brand that launched the fancy coffee drink phenomenon. Whether you are a coffee drinker or not, you know this company and can agree that it excels at its point of difference! The company always manages to hire truly friendly people, folks who know how to smile and are ready to make your beverage of choice and your day. The soft music played in the company's shops soothes the spirit, easing away the stress of a sometimes-hectic day. More than anything else, this retailer understands that when you walk into its stores, you are a guest. This point of difference ensures the customer's positive experience, and that leads to extensive repeat business—and huge financial growth for the company.

The Point of Difference for Your Prospect

When it comes to sharing the point of difference in your company or organization with a prospect, there are other essential aspects to examine. These include your compensation plan. Yes, even your compensation plan needs to have a point of difference. Are you thoroughly familiar with the plan your company offers? Do you know what your key selling points are? Can you communicate clearly and enthusiastically about bonuses, total payout, structure, and more?

Over the years, I have learned some crucial "ah-has" that have made the difference when it comes to inspiring a good prospect to join my organization. Here are a few suggestions that you may want to use depending on what company and type of plan you are currently promoting:

- We pay deep to allow for long-term growth and major residual income possibilities. Share the stories about your top earners with your prospects and explain how these top people are already achieving that sort of residual income.

- We pay on width because width leads to long-term growth. Again, use success stories to make your point, and remember to use this important phrase because it applies to your business as well as your prospects' future business: "Every time you sponsor a new person, it's as if you opened a new store in that person's city." For example, when you sponsor your friend Bob in Boise, Idaho, it's as if you just opened a new location for your business in Boise. When you sponsor Mary in Duluth, Minnesota, it's like you just broke ground for a booming new store in Duluth—it's all opportunity for distributing your products and growing your business network.

- We tailor our presentation to meet the perceived needs and desires of the prospect, whether the person wants to make millions of dollars or just an extra $1,000 a month. Know what speaks to the person to whom you are talking.

Perhaps your company has been paying both deep and on width for twenty years and has developed many millionaires as a result. This might even be the same compensation system that has developed many part-time people who are currently earning $1,000 per month part time. Depending on the person you're talking to, either example can make a positive impact.

However, if you are talking to someone who already earns a six-figure income, then the potential $1,000 per month won't attract them. They are already achieving a decent level of income. But what if they hate their job or loathe the long commute they face five to six days a week? Again, they aren't going to get very excited about an extra $1,000 a month, but they may find the stories about the big income quite tantalizing.

Now, there's a huge amount of people out there in your community who would bend over backwards for that extra $1,000 per month and who may not believe that they could ever earn a million dollars. How many are there out there? You'll find that out quickly when you start using some guerrilla marketing strategies.

With over 50 years in the business, Larry Thompson started in the 1960s when he was a hippie construction worker with no business knowledge or people skills. It never even occurred to him that he could do anything besides work with his hands. Here is his story:

> I went to my first meeting as a guest of someone who had been invited. Not only was it my first meeting, but it was also the first time I had ever been in a hotel! What I did have back then, however, were three critical assets needed in the MLM industry—desire, willingness, and teachability.
>
> In today's business climate, more emphasis is needed on encouraging and inspiring self-responsibility. To me, self-determination is an unwavering concept in MLM. It is one

constant skill required, with training tools and sales techniques simply the how-tos you use—and which may change over time. Remember: tools don't build houses; craftsmen build houses using the tools at their disposal.

There are the speed bumps to manage in this profession, but they are a fact of life. Train, do the work, and don't quit. You also must be prepared to accept that 80 percent of your people will be part-time. MLM is a tremendous industry for people who are like me when I first got started. You can get started with little money and no MLM skills, contacts, or experience. But, while it's easy to get someone excited about MLM initially, people are all too often eager to lie to themselves about potential positive results to feel good, only to lose traction over time.

The truth is that little steps forward yield those positive results you and your people want. Real success comes to people who have the desire, willingness, and teachability. This has made all the difference for me, and it can be the same for you.

Follow the Leader to Success

This final section dovetails perfectly with where we started—your point of difference. When you are the leader of a business or organization, your people want to know your point of difference, especially if you are the kind of leader who is there to assist them.

It's not enough simply to claim that you, your product, or your company is unique and special. Your prospects want to know that you can help them because you do or have something unique and/or can lead them in a way that is better for them and their success.

Remember, it's all about the prospect. You must convince your prospects that your points of difference will benefit them today, and in the long term. Here are some examples of conversational hooks that I use to express my commitment to my prospect and to our mutual success:

- "I'm looking for a new front-line person to develop a successful business over the next few months. I already have a good group now, and they all have been trained. I'm ready to build a new group with you if you are willing to commit."

- "I'm new too, but I will teach you everything I know. Remember that the company offers a training program as well, and I'll show you how to get involved. So, some things we may learn together at the same time, and that's great. That's also why we have weekly meetings here in [your city]."

- "I'll take some time every day to work directly with you and your people until you learn the business yourself. I will also assist you with a daily coaching call, three-way calls, or hold meetings face-to-face with you and your prospects. I will match your effort 100 percent. You work with me, and I'll work with you."

See how it works? Now, take your point of difference to the next level, and address what you think your prospect wants and how you can provide it:

What would your target consumer want to gain from your product? You can discover this by asking your current customers or asking members of your downline what they like best about your product. The more you can identify exactly what your prospects want to hear, the better chance you have of making the sale. Build your product identity around your ability to delight your customers to their absolute satisfaction.

Address the competition. Survey your competition to find out how they represent themselves to their prospects. Then take the next step and find out if the claims they make are true! Ask yourself: How do I distinguish myself as being a notch higher than the competition? Do I deliver better results? Are my products less expensive, more reliable, or better tasting? Pull away from the pack by using your competition as the measuring stick for how you can improve your own business.

Address perceptions. How does the public perceive your product, or your industry overall? Like it or not, you should accept people's generalizations and perceptions as truth. If someone thinks that network marketing is not a viable business, does that make it true? For that person, yes—because his or her perception is his or her reality. No matter what, always build yourself up as being the exception to the rule, and then demonstrate why.

Distinguish Your Points of Difference

To be truly successful in this business, you must promote yourself and your company as being responsible, credible, and better at what you do or offer than anyone else. How do you position yourself as a company that is a cut above the rest?

You saw it in this chapter: Identify yourself, your product, your company, and your business opportunity as a point of difference. Take whatever is unique and different and use it powerfully and responsibly to help others make the decision to join your team.

Focus on what consumers want. Focus on what your prospects want. Know the public perceptions of your business and your competitor's claims in intimate detail. Then, highlight your own points of difference and get ready to shine!

Chapter 7

GUERILLA MARKETING WITH LESS MONEY

Marketing your business is a necessary action step to building a successful, growing enterprise, but many people look at marketing and think, "buy a big newspaper ad" or "mail postcards to 10,000 people" without really looking at the big picture. Here's the reality check: Your potential customers and downline prospects are deluged every day with marketing for products and services that are newer, cheaper, and funded by deep-pocket advertising budgets.

So how do you stand out in the crowd? How do you generate big marketing results without breaking the bank? Guerilla marketing is perfect for the entrepreneur on a budget, and in a nutshell, it means having the moxie to think outside the box and apply creative, nontraditional, low-cost/no-cost tactics to build person-to-person relationships that drive your business growth.

Mind Your Marketing

It all starts with your attitude. The mind-set that has served me and my businesses well is that I see every activity and every encounter in my daily life as an opportunity to grow my business. Marketing my business doesn't get vacation days or time off, and why would it? I'm doing what I love, offering products, services, and wealth-building opportunities that serve my fellow human beings. Goodwill and good business sense are full-time trademarks of who I am as a person. This means that whether I'm having breakfast with a bunch of local businessmen, grabbing a quick latte at Starbucks, or taking my kids to the museum to see the dinosaurs, I look for the opportunity to sell my products or grow my downline.

Next, marketing is something that you must see as an investment in your business, and therefore, an investment in you. This doesn't mean that you must buy the biggest, fanciest ad in the Wall Street Journal or hire some big, crackerjack agency to market your message. It shouldn't cost you a fortune to promote your business. This may feel a little disconcerting for those of you coming from the corporate world of big budgets and the outsourcing of all the creative development, production, and distribution of your company's key messages. Direct sales brings with it a brave new marketing world, where you use that invaluable tool—called your brain—and invest your own time, energy, and creativity in your business.

Some of you may balk at being asked to be creative. If you're not sure what to do or fear that you're just not a creative thinker, talk with your upline. Your upline will want to share best practices with you, and these conversations can spark ideas. An online search for "guerilla marketing" will also help to percolate some ideas. Remember, I'm talking about unconventional, low-cost, or no-cost delivery of your business message.

Consider this example. A woman in my downline launched her direct-sales business with very little money to devote to marketing her products. She devised the idea of stamping her sales message and contact information on those small sticky message sheets we all buy by the pack. She left her "ad" wherever she went, and her sales message got out there—one peeled-off sheet at a time. Calls came in, and the constant flow of product sales kept her going as she grew her downline. How much did this unconventional marketing tactic cost? About $20 for a custom stamp and a bunch of sticky-note pads. If you check online, you'll find that custom-printed sticky notes are available too, and they will run you as low as fifty cents a pad with quantity orders.

Packaging Your Messages

As a distributor, you sell products to potential customers, and you market money-making opportunities to prospective downline people. These are two distinct talking points, and I've learned that it's important not to mix my messages.

When I'm selling my product, I stick to the features and benefits of the product. When I am recruiting a new downline person, I promote the benefits of becoming a multilevel marketing distributor.

This is true whether you're meeting someone face to face, or leaving tear sheets or flyers in the lobby of an apartment building. Mixing your messages diffuses the power of the message. We've all seen notices tacked onto telephone poles declaring something like, "Lose weight fast. Make $10,000 a month." If all someone has ever wanted to do is shed the thirty pounds that have plagued him or her for years, the first message will catch his or her attention, whereas the money-making message may make him or her ask, "What's the catch?" Remember, a happy customer who falls in love with your product becomes a perfect candidate for distributorship—when the time is right. Likewise, while the svelte owner of a yoga studio will want to know all about the viability of your weight-loss product, the promise of additional cash flow for his or her business probably will get his or her attention first.

When you're packaging your message, be sure to have a promotional hook. You know that business cards are a must because each one is a mini flyer that you carry with you and hand out all the time. So, whenever you're handing out your business card, placing an ad, or leaving a stack of sell sheets, make sure that there's a call to action. My business card, for example, always has a promotional theme, such as, "Buy one vitamin product and get 50 percent off the second item" or "Call me and you'll receive a coupon for a free skin-care product." Your goal is to make the customer want to have a conversation with you!

Seasonal campaigns also make perfect sense for certain products. If your product is for weight loss, you will want to market big at certain times of the year, such as right after the winter holidays or when spring is announcing the imminent return of bathing suit weather. Use both your creative intuition and common sense to package your messages and to time their arrival. If you need ideas or guidance, that's what your upline is for. These days, holiday sales promotions are expected. Things like Christmas. Boxing Day, Easter, Digital Friday, Cyber Monday, etc.

An idea I really like, is honoring different lines of work as a promotion. Firefighter Friday, Nurses' Day, etc. are all things that bring in business from people who are mostly underappreciated and overworked.

Using Success Stories

The use of customer endorsements is a powerful way to draw new customers and distributors. Your first step is to ask your upline compliance person about company guidelines because permissions may be required to use a customer's story or images. Once you have the green light, ask satisfied customers to write or email you a testimonial about how your product or service has benefited their lives or their businesses.

If you market a diet plan, nutritionals, or skin-care products, the use of before and after pictures is a bonus. Nothing sells a product better than proven results! And if those results are promoted through a celebrity voice, that's a license to print money.

Success stories can be used in your promotional literature, on your website, and in presentations. This is where you want to take a page from the "winners' handbook." Talk with your upline about ideas that have yielded great returns.

One of the men I currently work with, has compiled an online file with over 160 pages of product testimonials. Jamie Hawley, a successful leader in his company, has kept the stories of many world-class, as well as, professional athletes who have benefited from his product. Jamie is "armed for bear" when someone asks about their product.

Tools You Can Use

Let's look at some of the valuable and cost-effective marketing techniques that I continue to use with these guerilla marketing guidelines:

- Think outside the box to stand out.
- Invest your time, money, and imagination in you.

- Stay true to your chosen message.

- Remain consistently loyal to your promotional theme.

- Choose methods that are low cost or no cost.

Warmed Up and Ready to Pitch

We've all heard the term elevator pitch, and having a creative, concise speech that is ready to use is your first "power tool." This quick (thirty seconds or less) conversation starter with the stranger on the elevator, the person in line with you at the grocery store, or the fellow business person at a seminar is your opportunity to get your message across.

Now, when using your elevator pitch, what you are selling is the appointment. You want the person to take your card or pamphlet and take some later action. If he or she is game to learn more right away, that's great. You also can hand the person your card and ask if he or she wants to meet for coffee or breakfast the next day. It's about the appointment. Your pitch is designed to grab people's attention and provide them with an action step.

Many companies have used "Want to lose weight? Ask me how" for years because it works. I've approached a prospect in an elevator with, "I'm looking for ten people who want to lose thirty pounds or more. Do you know anybody I could talk to?" Whether the individual I'm talking to is a member of the target audience for my product or my new messenger for a future product sale, it's all good. He or she walks away with some of my marketing information, and the people with whom he or she shares the information can become my customers.

Try out your pitches and see what works for you. This tool is one of the easiest to test your market and learn what's truly effective. You'll know that what you're saying is working for you when you find a potential customer chatting with you as you walk off the elevator, or agreeing to have coffee with you later. And if all that happens is that you have an opportunity to hand someone your business card, you've taken a step toward growing your business.

Just Show Up

In this business, where person-to-person communication makes all the difference, networking is one of the most valuable tools in your marketing tool belt. You've got to show up where potential customers and distributors meet, and this means joining every networking group you can find. Get out there and meet people. Shake as many hands as you can and share your message.

There are numerous business-related groups to use, such as BNI, Toastmasters Anonymous, and Women in Business, as well as hometown organizations such as the Rotary Club, Lions Club, and your local Chamber of Commerce. One of my local business groups holds a monthly 7:00 a.m. breakfast meeting, where members are invited to present a one-minute "commercial" about their business. You can bet I'm there ready to pitch. I also capitalize on any chance I get to mix a meeting with a meal. If a business group get-together like this provides breakfast or lunch, it's a perfect opportunity to invite a prospect to talk about the benefits of my product or becoming a distributor, and my message is heard by others at the table.

Other networking opportunities include groups that revolve around your special interests or where you know other successful people will be. Support your museums, concert halls, zoos, and other centers of culture, and you'll find hundreds of men and women ready to hear your pitch. And you get to enjoy amazing artwork or fine music while you're building your business.

If the price of admission that you're looking for is "free," you'll find such a deal at the various informational seminars we all learn of. About once a month I get an invitation in the mail to attend a free special event to learn about exciting new opportunities in real estate, setting up a retirement fund, drawing a living will, or other service. Talk about a captive audience for your message! Everyone who attends these events has money on their minds, and you get the chance to hand out your business card and chat up your products or your business.

Trade shows, business fairs, expos—these are all golden opportunities to mingle with possible customers. Get used to seeing every gathering of human beings as a chance to grow your business. Go to those seminars and free workshops. Watch for local shops and businesses hosting an open house. Attend lectures, parties, and political events. Show up, share your message and materials, and your marketing efforts will generate real results.

Your Ad Here

Placing ads in newspapers is a marketing method that I can enthusiastically recommend as long as you or members of your downline avoid what many network marketing novices want to do: run a big, splashy one-time ad in your newspaper that could cost you thousands of dollars. Instead, consider an inexpensive classified ad in a local paper or in one of those free specialty newspapers that consumers love to grab; such an ad can be both effective and cost-effective. Remember to consider your local ethnic or foreign-language press, too. Growing your downline in multicultural communities means reaching people through the periodicals they read. This strategy has been extremely rewarding for me, because downline people with personal or business connections in other countries have been responsible for much of the global reach my business now enjoys.

When it comes to shopping around for the best ad rates, use an ad sales rep. Newspapers are hungry for your advertising dollars, so ask the rep to make the proposition worth your while. Once you've decided which media outlets to use for your advertising, build a relationship there. A little-known secret in media relations is that newspapers are sometimes willing to write a small feature article on a loyal advertiser, and the ad sales rep often can help make this happen. An article on you and your business in your local newspaper means free publicity—and extended reach for your messages.

Ads are also a good tool for co-op marketing. If your city's most popular pizza parlor allows you to put a bunch of flyers by the cash register, talk to the owner about an ad that promotes both businesses. He or she may agree to pay for part of the ad if you offer a coupon for a free second pizza to everyone who calls you about your product.

Getting Ahead with Leave-Behinds

Whether you decide to go with a three-fold pamphlet or a one-sided, one-color sell sheet about your product, your local print shop can help you put together a cost-effective marketing tool, often helping with the design and layout at very affordable rates. A good printer will want to help you be successful. While prices can vary, I've typically spent about $100 for 1,000 flyers. Great printing rates are available through online companies, but you may sacrifice some of the personal attention you get with your local shop.

Besides leaving a stack of flyers on a display table at your networking group or next to the cash register at your neighborhood convenience mart, there are dozens of creative ways to use these tools. It's illegal to leave flyers on car windshields, but you can stick them on vending machines, by public phones, on community bulletin boards in your grocery store, and in residential door jambs.

If you walk your dog every evening, why not take along 100 flyers and distribute them along your route? It's good for you, and it's good for Fido. I've used this tactic for years, and it has sold products and helped me to build my downline.

Today, my marketing budget allows me to produce small, low-cost CDs and DVDs to get my messages out. Every time I go to the gym, I leave a mini-CD in five or six different lockers. That's a large enough number of CD placements to generate some valuable leads and a small enough number of leave-behinds to avoid irritating the health club management staff.

You produce flyers to build your business, and your goal is to build your business wherever you go. So why not use the businesses you frequent in your daily life? Most of us use a dry cleaner, a hair salon or barber shop, a place for getting the oil changed in our car, and myriad other retail outlets. Take a dry-cleaning establishment, for example. When I take in my dry cleaning, I make it a point to meet the owner or manager, tell him or her about my product, and ask if I can leave a stack of flyers by the cash register or place a drop box for a drawing where someone can win a free sample. If the answer is no, I take my dry-cleaning business to another establishment and try again.

Take, for example, my friend Juan. Juan works with a company that markets weight-loss products and has product tear sheets placed in many dry cleaners, laundromats, and even a few restaurants in my area. I spoke to him recently, and he shared with me a "sell point" on his tear sheets that has worked quite successfully for him. He pinpoints that a person can continue to occasionally eat unhealthy food and still be able to lose weight. He even spends time at some of these establishments and shows around his before and after photos. Remember, results tell the story better than anything.

It's in the Mail

I use direct-mail campaigns, even in this internet age and even though I know that a certain percentage of my postcards will land in the trash or get lost in the mail. If your budget allows it, opt for printing a larger postcard so that the recipient will notice it, and make sure that your mailer has that promotional hook. Not only does this motivate prospective customers to call you, but it also gives you an opportunity to measure the success of your campaign.

When it comes to direct mail—and advertising as well—my rule of thumb is to promote big and test small. You're using your own money to create promotional tools that carry a big impact without a big price tag and, therefore, you'll want to measure to see if a marketing tactic actually works for you. I often co-produce flyers with other members of my downline because this amortizes the cost of production and allows for a wider range of distribution. If ten of us go in together on a bulk order and we only get three call backs among us, it's clear that the campaign is a bust. Check with your upline people. It's a safe bet that they have done direct-mail campaigns before, and you should be able to produce a mailer based on their past market research.

Once again, it's tempting to want to produce something fancy and expensive. I prefer to choose quantity over quality. If my postcard says what it needs to say in a compelling way, and the message has the chance to hit 10,000 potential customers, the chance of making sales is far greater.

Where you find those potential customers for your direct-mail piece is also important to think through. Membership groups often will allow you to purchase a membership list, and you'll want to know if the group has any prohibitive guidelines. You also can buy mailing lists from various sources, but this suggestion comes with a caveat; if you see a sales ad that says something like "10,000 for $89"— caveat emptor! This operation may be using offshore servers to store illegally obtained contact information. If it sounds too good to be true, it probably is.

Doing Double Duty

You may deal with downline people who have a full-time job or consulting business and who run their network marketing business part time. Someone with a sales job, for example, is in front of potential customers or new distributors every day—how can he or she work in the direct-sales message while honoring the contract to market the products or services of the full-time job? The salesperson represents two separate businesses, and I recommend keeping them separate. I would conduct one meeting, and when it is done, I would bring up the direct-sales message. It could be presented as an "Oh, by the way" after conclusion of the regular business, where the business owner is presented with a flyer, a CD, or a DVD about the direct-sales business. If possible, take a ten-minute mental break before changing the subject.

Try a Test Team

You'll be using a mix of elevator pitches, promotion-driven business cards, direct-mail offers, and ads to market your business, and measuring results will be easy. If you get a handful of responses that are a bridge to nowhere, you'll need to rethink the message, your method, or both. I like to engage a test team for many of my marketing strategies, where great minds choose a market and a strong branding statement, and we see what positive results we can generate.

Choosing a new market can be as easy as asking your downline if they have any contacts there. The markets that my team selects usually offer a special hook of their own—such as "home of this year's Super Bowl champions"—or where there's strong representation of a certain ethnic population. If we have a news sports drink to promote, for example, we can use the "Super Bowl winners" hook for our message in that city.

We choose our market and our theme, and then we "go to town" marketing our message. Sometimes that term is figurative, and we use purchased lists, online tools, direct mail, and other tools to recruit new customers and distributors long distance. Other times, we literally go to that town, and one or more members of the test team temporarily relocates there.

There are also times when you have a new market opened to you by invitation. You probably attend conferences and conventions that are held in cities outside your general area, and these new markets are prime pickings for expanding your business. If you're going to be in Scottsdale for several days, use your marketing toolkit to warm the market before you go, and then travel to Scottsdale one or two weeks early and follow up on your leads. And if it's an event related to your business, you already know that the top leadership will be there. Use the news that they'll be there to attract new prospects in advance, and then use those big names in your business to help close the deal.

This is a concept called 'window dressing,' and it works. Remember, success breeds success, so people want to see and hear from other people earning big money in your business. Think of it like a beautiful storefront with a great window display. Because the display is attractive, you're drawn to enter the store (or the business in this case). I've been amazed over the years by how many people have told me that the first meeting they were ever invited to was one where I was the speaker and that they happily became involved after my talk. This is an example of people promoting their upline properly and using window dressing to its full advantage.

Do-it-Yourself Marketing

It's clear that marketing your business on a budget means packaging concise, creative promotional messages that reach your audiences effectively, and doing this in a world that floods all of us with sales messages every day. It's not easy, it's hands-on work, and it's necessary for the success of your business.

Regardless of which tool you use or how much you spend, these tools have one purpose: to open the door to a person-to-person conversation. From the elevator pitch to the classified ad, the purpose of your marketing efforts is to sell the appointment— that golden opportunity to communicate in depth with another human being about how your product enhances people's lives or how network marketing's earning potential can improve someone's way of life. Simply put, marketing opens the door to being of service, and that's what network marketing is all about.

Chapter 8

BUILDING YOUR BUSINESS WITH THE INTERNET

The World Wide Web has radically altered the landscape of business, allowing us to communicate in real-time and to market to countless people across the globe. You now can reach potential customers and distributors on a massive scale, achieving numbers far beyond what you can generate in a meeting over coffee.

While network marketing is primarily a personal, face-to-face business, it's tough to deny the power of the Web. There are members of my own downline who have used the internet masterfully to build dynamic downlines around the world, generating tens of thousands of dollars in monthly revenue via electronic marketing. These people know the secret to building business using the internet; no matter what the technology, human beings must be engaged and supported. It's not as easy as just getting a list of prospects, sending out an email blast, and watching the checks come in. If you're looking to get rich quick by selling online, you're better off buying a lottery ticket.

This is probably why internet marketing frustrates many people. They don't know what to do, and they don't understand the real goal. By developing an online atmosphere of trust and relationship, you can use the internet to transform what we call a "cold" market into a warm, engaging market—and that takes time, effort, and patience.

Most of us start in direct sales by looking to build our downline close to home. Friends, family members, and business associates already know and trust us, so the message can focus more immediately on the products or financial opportunity. When you send out an email to a fresh list, however, your online contacts may not know you from Adam or have any personal history with you or your products. They also might not easily differentiate between you and the gazillions of other virtual voices they encounter every day in their flooded email boxes. Your message could even end up in their spam folder. This means that you must use online marketing to build a mentoring system that truly engages people. You need to gradually deepen relationships, shoring up trust and loyalty over time, and continually adding value to your contacts' online experience of you and your message.

Educated Contacts Mean Business

People in the know about online marketing have long realized that the internet is a communications and advertising tool to attract and educate prospects. An educated, well-qualified lead that you've nurtured over time is always a better prospect for your business. So, you begin with a list of business-oriented contacts, and you educate them over time about your products or services. You make value-added business tools available to them, maintain an e-conversation with them, earn their trust, and then—and only then—make them an offer.

This process could take weeks, months, or even a couple of years with some prospects as they read your email messages, try some products, and review your materials. Have patience. Whatever you do, don't rush the offer or bombard new prospects with too much information right off the bat. Eventually, when you do make the offer, you're bound to have more hits because your prospects are informed, and you have more prospects to make offers to because you've built a substantial list of qualified businesspeople.

Remember this fundamental fact: While you can use the internet to build a large organization by collecting and connecting contacts, you don't really do the sponsoring online. This fact shouldn't surprise you. Network marketing is a personal business, right? My internet-savvy downline people make their offers by phone using the necessary personal touch—and by this time, their prospects are waiting to hear from them.

While I am far from being an internet marketing pro, I can give you a few stories of success I have had in using the internet and Facebook to do the following:

1. warm up an existing contact.

2. eventually recruit and retain that contact long term.

3. use a drip information tactic to build with that contact in his market.

You have already read Don and Pam Hutchinson's story in Chapter 1. They were friends of mine from a prior MLM company where I was their upline. I also knew about their success with a prior company that dates to the early 1980s, when both the Hutchinsons and I were newbies in the industry. Anyway, one day in 2011, I was having a meeting with one of the executives in our current company. We got talking about our then smallest market, which we were opening in the UK and Ireland. We agreed I would set out to contact a few people in this market that we had yet to really develop. Of course, I thought of Don and Pam, and wondered aloud what they were doing. I went home and sent an instant message to them via Facebook, as well as two other people I knew in the UK. Don wrote back a few days later and said they had retired to the south of Spain. However, as both had an interest in health, they would be interested in hearing about my product.

I started to drip information, both verbally as well as supported by studies, etc., about my product. After about a month of emails, instant messages, and a couple Skype calls, we decided to ship some samples to the Hutchinson's address in Northern Ireland, as they would be visiting there shortly. Finally, once they tried the product, they knew they wanted to use it. This still took a couple months. Even though they had "retired," a once-successful MLMer can't resist a new opportunity if the case is strong enough. The next part of the drip was an invite to them to our home office to "kick the tires." We did this, and the Hutchinson's have been a major leader in our business ever since. They have built a nice business in the UK and Ireland and will surely have another when our company expands to Spain.

A few points to consider:

1. Constantly review who's on your Facebook, Instagram, etc.

2. Where do they live?

3. Be okay with getting a customer first. Great customers like Don and Pam eventually may transition to business builder if they want to.

4. Drip on lots of people, with a little information at a time.

Internet Marketing Basics

So, you're raring to go with an internet strategy to grow your downline, but you're in the dark about how to get started. Your first step is to check with your upline people to see what they've been doing by way of internet marketing, and what they have to offer your new business. In the world of direct sales, you're going to find that some successful businesses have been built on nothing more technical than the telephone, whereas others use every online bell and whistle available.

We also must be sensitive to the varied levels of comfort and experience people have with using the web. We all know bright, business-minded people who can barely turn on their computers, let alone send emails. Internet technology is a valuable tool, and its value is building exponentially every year. Smart marketers know that they can't choose to be left behind on the technology end, but this doesn't mean that we all must become a bunch of geeks. It just means that you and your downline will need to know what, when, why, and how to use it. Think 'technology with a purpose.'

Internet marketing starts with a website, and you will need one. Now, before you go out and spend thousands of dollars having a website built, there are other, more cost-effective solutions. For starters, your upline already may have a tremendous website, where you can get your own branded marketing page. This not only saves you money, but it also lets you benefit in less tangible ways. If you are new to the business and have no personal brand power, you can bet that your company's top leaders have cultivated a real brand cache. When you link your webpage to their website, you get to borrow some of their glow, drawing power, and personal touch, while you build up your brand and your own story until it is big enough to tell. Another outstanding benefit of linking your webpage or website to branded host websites is that you'll often be able to buy leads from them, paying for qualified leads that you can contact by email or by phone.

Here's one way to accumulate people to talk to:

Facebook Fan Pages: These are what they sound like. Fan pages allow people to follow you and become fans of both you and your business. This is a great way to accumulate contacts as well as "fans" of yourself. This is much more personal than just having a regular Facebook account, by the way.

Once you have your plan for a website or fan page in place, you'll want to investigate other online tools such as webinar host companies, and how to offer video training. There are also industry blogs, e-newsletters, and other informational offerings—all designed to help you attract more people who will want to buy your product or join your business. And once you've drawn someone to your website, you'll want to capture his or her contact information. The best way to do this is to offer something of value that motivates the visitor to fill out a contact form. We'll get into this later in the chapter.

The Zoom Room: I was in Monterrey, Mexico a few years back and my good friend, Adriana Cazares, had some people she wanted to introduce to me in another part of the country. That day I was introduced to Zoom and it helped change my thinking. Why? I had used many online meetings but fell in love with Zoom because we could all see one another and interact. Since that time, I've done meetings all over the world with this technology. Sometimes, I even use my cell phone to do a zoom call. I can be in a restaurant or airport and still see the people I'm working with. Many of our leaders use it for weekly calls and opportunity meetings. Get familiar with it, as it is a modern tool you need in your tool belt and is easy to use.

See Results with SEO

You've probably heard the terms search engine optimization (SEO) and search engine marketing (SEM). They allow you to use popular and powerful online tools that, while not all free, are cost-effective and very useful when it comes to driving prospects to your website. Basically, you want your web copy to hold keywords that are specific to how someone would search for your products or business. Search engines, such as Google and Yahoo, have methods for analyzing websites and logging what words are used most often, which is what makes using SEO so important to the success of your online business.

Then, you move on to SEM and ad words, of which Google Ad Words is an excellent example. Here, you pay for the ability to submit keywords to Google that best represent how a prospect might search for your business online. These ad words run twenty-four hours a day, seven days a week, and they can dramatically increase the probability of directing a web-surfing prospect to your website over others with similar offerings. The other good news is that you only pay for the searches that end up visiting your website.

You also can consider sponsored online advertisements for your business, such as the ones you see on the right side of the screen when you view your search results. Sponsored online ads can be especially worthwhile if you team with an upline person who already has an established, branded website. You split the ad costs and get your fair share of the leads generated by the ad.

About Funded Sponsorship

Let's say that you're someone with a job who has entered the exciting business of network marketing on a part-time basis. It's relatively easy at first for you to budget some of your paycheck towards marketing your direct-sales business. Once you see that your marketing efforts are yielding some results, however, you'll get that urge to up your efforts so that you can really build your downline and make more money each month. How will you do this? Is it wise or even practical to think about working harder or logging more hours at your day job just so that you can fund your direct-sales marketing strategy?

The answer is no, and this is what brings us to the option of funded sponsorship. Funded sponsorship involves a value-added product that makes you money before you start selling your featured product or service or even talk about your business. You know that you're not going to sell your product or distributor opportunity to 100 percent of your list. However, everyone wants information on how to make more money, and what you're selling with funded sponsorship is information on how to do just that.

The for-purchase informational material, in the form of a downloadable document, an eBook, or a training course, appeals to your prospects' core desire to make money. The information-based affiliate business helps to build your prospect list while funding your advertising budget. What you have is a noncompetitive side business that generates additional revenues—and these profit dollars allow you to market your direct sales business more effectively, more consistently, and buy leads for your list.

Will all the buyers of your "how to make money" materials purchase your network marketing company's products or join your downline? Probably not. Many individuals will buy your general online materials and ride off happily into the sunset. But you'll recruit some of them, and those who do not join your business likely will become referral engines for you. Most successful businesses I know use funded sponsorship, and who can blame them? They are fostering the growth of their business without shelling out of pocket for marketing funds. Their advertising is paying for itself.

Making Sense of Social Media

When it comes to meeting and engaging potential customers on their own online turf, social media offers you a powerful competitive advantage—and as they say, if you're not in there providing answers, your competition is. Social media follows much of the same rules as other internet marketing tools, only interactive participation is increased exponentially. Traditional marketing has long fallen into the category of "Here's my message. Come buy my product." The new world of social media takes marketing into the realm of the conversation. People come together on social media sites such as Facebook, Twitter, Myspace, and Instagram to name a few.

Here's a second Facebook concept I've used and a funny story at that. My last name, as best we can tell, has its origins back in Germany in the 1400s. Again, as best we can tell, our common ancestors with the Solleder last name all go back to this little area of Wurzburg. That being the case, in one way, shape or form, everyone with this last name is related. How far removed no one knows and for this story for MLM it doesn't matter. I started contacting everyone on Facebook several years ago. Found relatives in many parts of the world including Peru. I have had ongoing conversations with several of my relatives in Peru about my company and product ever since. At this time, it looks like my long lost cousins will be joining our business when we open in the fall. What's even more interesting is that they speak only Spanish. I brought in one of my Spanish leaders to help them get started and we have had several Zoom meetings.

Have you ever Facebooked or Googled your last name? Bet you have similar relatives that might have an interest in your business. This search is at least a great way to build the family tree and is a fun thing to do and share with your kids and grandkids.

P.S. I've even done ancestry.com to find some additional long-lost family members. Once again, fun and interesting. I found out I'm partly from Norway. Fun stuff!

LinkedIn to Form and Join Communities and to Share and Discover Information

One of the most common mistakes people in our industry make is to create a profile on Facebook or Twitter, upload a video on YouTube, and then sit back and wait for the orders to pour in. This is like building a house ten miles out of town and then sitting there waiting for someone to invite you into town for dinner—isn't going to happen. You need to drive into town, shake hands with the townspeople, share who you are and what you're about, and listen to the stories of the residents who've lived there a while.

Once you join one of the social media sites, your best bet is to spend some time exploring the dialogues that pertain to your business. You begin by searching through keywords and then observing the conversations. When you find a community that fits your products or services, you participate through the exchange of information. Whatever you do, forget about anything like a hard sell! Anyone barging into a group with a pushy marketing agenda, disrupting the natural flow of the conversation, is usually met with distrust or anger. You wouldn't walk into a dinner party with new friends and start yelling out, "So, who here wants to lose thirty pounds?" The same rules of social conduct apply here. Your goal is to bring value to the conversation—not as a salesperson but as a human being.

Remember, too, that the communities you join are typically quite diverse. Just as your local Starbucks community is typically a wonderful blend of social demographics, your social media network will be even more so. After all, social media culture is a global culture. Your messages need to be clear and beneficial to all members, which makes real information and customer testimonials invaluable.

As you engage, you are marketing yourself as much as your business. This makes transparency crucial—and that means that everything you post, tweet, upload, and say is public domain. Everything you communicate online through social media sites can be discovered and indexed by search engines.

Social media processes can seem overwhelming and time-consuming at first, but once you learn the tools, the benefits to you and your business can be significant. Find out who in your upline is already using social media and go to school studying them. Once you're active in your own Facebook or LinkedIn community, you'll be able to share your own observations on what works to build your customer base or distributor downline.

Drilled down to its most basic essence, social media channels are all about building online relationships, and the benefits are trust, friendship, and brand loyalty. Just as it takes time to build relationships in the real world, the online world of Twitter or Facebook—or any of the other social media sites appearing on an ever-growing list—requires the same patience, sincerity, and person-to-person engagement.

Going Global Using the Internet

Thanks to the Internet, you now can select markets for your business just about anywhere you want. While not all markets are "open," there are over 160 countries that welcome network marketing enterprises with open arms. Going global doesn't mean that you have to go to that country, but then again, there's nothing wrong with holding a training session on a veranda in Costa Rica. What you'll need to do is build a presence. The general network marketing rule about the internet still applies on the international front. The Web is simply a connection tool for person-to-person communications. Just because you're selling products to someone in New Zealand or enrolling a distributor in Brazil doesn't mean that you let up for an instant on maintaining the personal touch.

My friend Jeff Weisberg is busy building a business in South America by using technology touches to make initial contact and connections with people there. As you'll learn from him, the process may start with the digital world, but the world of MLM is ultimately a face-to-face business.

I started in MLM at age 19, having been influenced by an entrepreneurial father who taught me a lot about residual income and sales. As soon as I saw what my lifestyle could be in direct sales, I dropped my plans to become an accountant and never looked back. For more than five years, I have been the single father of two young boys, and the MLM lifestyle has given me what no conventional job or business could; being there for my boys, raising them, working from home while coaching their sports teams, and even taking them on business trips.

Even now, as my friend Jeff's boys are in university, he's able to include them in his business, and allows them to share not only in the prosperity of his business but also the many business trips to see the world.

The internet is a powerful tool for our industry, and it has both positives and negatives. Social media, for example, is a great way to meet and connect with people and to impart information, but it is hard to keep people in your business if they only know you from a social media site. Retention requires having conversations and in-person communication. In fact, about 78 percent of all MLM business is conducted face to face (www.dsa.org).

Email blasts are also great with an established group you've built because they take less time and effort. But to think that this tool is a way to recruit and keep people without ever meeting them is a mistake. People buy you. That's why big events are important to us. They are the "glue"—the place where people get to put faces to names.

I am busy building a business in Columbia now, using email, social media, webinars, and other technology to make initial connections. But I am also traveling down there to meet these people personally. The internet and the other communication technologies we have today are the gateways to what really builds your business—face-to-face meetings.

Creating a warm market overseas means using the same simple expansion model you're using domestically. Your internet-based communications will still be grounded in educating, and building trust and loyalty with business-minded individuals over time. While meeting for coffee or holding in-home training meetings will be a challenge until you've enrolled a local downline team that can manage the process, you can still hold webinars and draw people to on-screen video training for step-by-step tutorials. The internet lets you build a team in a distant location by offering a motivational haven of support online.

Much of the time, the online ads that are most effective for you in Philadelphia or Toronto will also work overseas. Members of my downline and I have chosen a foreign market and run both print and online ads to drum up product sales and attract prospective distributors. It takes a little initial research and quite possibly a trip there for one or more members of our team, but mainstream international markets have proven to be prime territory for building new networks for our businesses.

Finally, the funded-sponsorship model works extremely well when you choose to target an international market, because the desire to make money crosses nearly all geographic and cultural boundaries. Use the internet to investigate the business messages common to your target country and what businesses are available there. Tailor your message.

Whether you buy an ad or an email list, you'll still offer an attractive value proposition via your informational materials, and from there, you'll build local contacts who can build your downline where they live—while you mentor them from your own backyard.

So, I've shared a few personal stories here but here's the universal appeal of the internet. You can't argue with the numbers. As of June 2019, here are the latest numbers, which are growing daily.

Facebook-over 2.3 billion monthly users

YouTube-over 1.9 billion monthly users

WhatsApp-1.5 billion monthly users

Messenger-1.3 billion monthly users

WeChat-1.06 billion monthly users

Instagram-1 billion monthly users

And those are the top, with many more being created. If you speak a second language you may find one or more just for your language. If you have a special interest, you will find some designed for that special interest.

Twitter—who can deny the power of Twitter in recent political elections, for example? Love or hate the candidates using Twitter, there is no denying its special place in communicating messages.

Another way many people are using to communicate is Facebook Live, a great technology to communicate from a live event such as a business opportunity meeting, convention or even first meeting with a friend who is joining your business today.

My experience with WhatsApp began this last year, when I created individual groups that I work with in many different markets. Some of these groups are focusing on specific things in markets or, in some cases, have nothing to do with MLM. However, WhatsApp is a great tool both for the written communication as well as the phone communication process.

Chapter 9

WHAT FAILURE TEACHES US

When I was about sixteen years old, my friend Greg mentioned that someone had offered to buy his father's business. Where I grew up, few people owned their own businesses. Most everyone worked for someone else. So, I was curious about Greg's dad. You could almost always find him outside tinkering with engines, and I guess most people thought that he was a mechanic. One afternoon I went over there, and Greg's father and I got to talking. He told me that when all his friends and relatives had reminded him that he had an engineering degree—and that he should get a "regular job"—he had gone against the grain and continued to labor on as an inventor.

After some financially unsuccessful patents, he'd eventually developed an additive that became very popular in the trucking industry. Greg's dad shared some wisdom that I still hold sacred today. He said, "When people told me to quit, I persisted. I focused even more. If there's one thing I can tell you, it's never listen to people who will steal your dreams." Two other things he shared also have stayed with me: "Never work for anyone but yourself" and "Don't be afraid to fail."

Take as an example my friend of over 20 years, Genece Miller. Genece had many reasons not to do well. She started a young family as a single mom, with kids who had lots of time demands.

What attracted you to MLM?

I liked the idea of being my own boss, being able to work when I wanted to, around my own schedule. I could do it part-time at first and replace my full-time income eventually. I wanted extra income, on my own terms. I worked hard and many hours for somebody else, I wanted to work smart and create my own wealth.

What has MLM meant to you?

To me, taking part in this great industry has meant so much. It gave me my life back. I truly feel that before I made the great decision to join the industry, I felt like someone else's puppet. I was not in control of my own life. I had so many people and elements to handle, I simply had no time and too many bosses.

I made a very strong and conscious decision to move forward; I didn't look back. I cut the cords and made a commitment to myself that I would do whatever it takes. I had no real experience in this industry, but I trusted the person who invited me to look at this business model and my mentors. It has truly changed my life for the better. It not only gave me a better life, it gave me a whole new perception on the way life can be. Now I wake up when I am finished sleeping. I don't set an alarm, unless I have a plane to catch or a special appointment I chose to make.

Because of this great decision I was able to be a stay-at-home mom—a single, stay-at-home mom because I was able to be the boss of me!

How do you see your future?

The future is bright! It is paved with opportunity....there truly are no limits except the ones you place upon yourself. Your life is a choice, you can guide it in the direction you desire. You will need to get in touch with your desires and set your goals. You can take baby steps or run fast and hard. The future is in your own hands. How wonderful is that?

I see an extremely rewarding future. As I help others learn how they too can be in control of their own destiny, it brings me joy.

Remember to dream big dreams; small dreams have no magic!

Living with Failure

When I was a young man, I was a sore loser. I didn't handle it well when my team lost a sporting event, when I got a poor grade on a test, or even when I missed a hole-in-one at miniature golf. That attitude carried over to my first network marketing venture. I had trouble accepting when people said no. The experience of rejection in direct sales has taught me a thing or two over the years.

First off, failure is not final. Just because someone says 'no' today doesn't mean that it's permanent. When they say 'no,' what they are really saying is, "I need to know more before I can say yes" or "It's not for me right now." Bear in mind that the fortune is in the follow-up. People's circumstances are changing constantly. I have learned to keep those prospects in a file that I can refer to three months, six months, or even a year later. There have been people I have worked on for years to join me in my business. Some of them came when the timing was right for them, and some have not come in yet; but I don't plan to give up on them.

Right Time, Right Fit

By the time you circle back to people you talked to weeks or even months ago, they may have recently lost their job. Maybe, like many people, they will have seen their financial portfolios decrease or disappear. They may now realize that retirement just got a lot farther away. They might be bored and want something new to stimulate them. They could be getting divorced and need a fresh start. It is always worth checking in with people to see where they are in their lives and whether the opportunity might be a good fit this time around.

Another thing I've learned from rejection is to fail forward. That is, study what you might have done wrong, and correct course. In the arena of athletic or artistic performance, the camera is always running. We can replicate that in the network marketing world. Have someone record your speeches, seminars, and two-on-one and one-on-one meetings. Ask yourself, what could I have done better? What sales aids should I have used? What might I have said to clinch the deal? What questions did the prospect ask that I wasn't prepared for?

I once gave a presentation to a senior-level manager of a large corporation. He seemed interested but didn't bite. The next day I called his home office. He was surprisingly glad to hear from me. I said, "Joe, what did I do wrong that you didn't join my business?" His explained that he found it rude that I was twenty minutes late and then didn't apologize. He suggested that I be more careful with other people's time. Even though he liked me and thought I would be very successful, he felt that I needed to learn that lesson. You probably can guess that I haven't been late for a meeting or conference call since.

Confronting Failure

We are all going to confront rejection at some time, especially in direct sales. It's what we do with the experience of failure that counts. I often link lessons about failure to the story of Dan Gable, an iconic wrestler. In 1972, I saw Gable win an Olympic gold medal in freestyle wrestling. In an interview with Frank Gifford, Gable reflected on his one and only wrestling loss. Throughout high school and college at Iowa State, he had never lost a single match. Gable headed into his final college match against a guy named Larry Owings from the University of Washington with a 182 to 0 record. He lost to Owings 13 to 11.

Despite all his victories to that point, Gable experienced a tremendous soul-searching. He acted and doubled his already intense training regimen to seven hours and participated in the Munich Olympics, where he didn't allow a single point to be scored against him. This feat is comparable to a baseball pitcher throwing six back-to-back no-hitters or a basketball player scoring 100 points a game in six straight games.

Was it the greatest sporting feat ever? I don't know. For me, it's definitely up there. To this day, though, in countless interviews, Gable still talks about that loss to Larry Owings. I don't know if the Owings match made him a better wrestler, but I do know that it helped him to sharpen his axe, leaving nothing to chance. And the results at Munich were superb. Gable also went on to lead the University of Iowa to over fifteen NCAA championships as head coach, and to coach many individual national, world, and Olympic champions. Any leader in sports, business, or personal development can take the lesson of Dan Gable to heart: success is about commitment, and failure is a powerful catalyst.

Another great role model I met a few years back is Fran Tarkenton. Fran was a quarterback for both the New York Giants and the Minnesota Vikings. Tarkenton went to the Super Bowl several times, each time coming out on the short end. But Fran never gave up. He always had a winning attitude, great desire, and a mind for business. While still playing football, Fran was already developing winning business ventures for the days when his football career was finished. He also wrote a terrific book on small-business development entitled, "What Losing Taught Me About Winning." In his book he talks about some of the challenges of financing a small business and some of the problems of starting from scratch with little capital. What happens when you lose, be it on the field or in the boardroom? How do you handle it? It's all about how you handle it and how failure shouldn't handle you.

Amazing Stories also from the World of Sports

Tom Brady, the 6th round pick and 166th in the NFL draft went on to set every record imaginable as an NFL quarterback. His high school JV team went an entire season without winning a game or scoring a touchdown. He was 7th on the depth chart at Michigan. (I wonder how the 6 guys ahead are doing?) Fast forward to today; Tom Brady just won his 6th Super Bowl at the age of 41! What if he had quit?

Michael Jordan didn't make his high school team and just kept working and working and working. Today Michael Jordan is not only one of, if not the greatest player in history, but has built many great businesses and is a billionaire!

NEVER, EVER QUIT ON YOURSELF!!!

Lessons from Direct-Sales Winners

When I began in network marketing, I had a little success early on but then hit a brick wall shortly after. I stopped doing the things that had given me the early success. I thought I would manage my group as opposed to bringing more people into the group. The slump caused me to think about quitting several times, especially when my income went the wrong way. However, what I realized was that for me to be successful, I had to get more people.

Over time, I learned that bringing in new people is like starting a new relationship. It is fun for a while, and the excitement is back every time new people come onboard. The key lesson from my time of failure is: always sponsor new people, at least one person a month, who you really want to work with.

Your business will never get stale because the contact capital of your new person will allow you to meet new people who are joining the business. This keeps you growing instead of "managing" your downlines, and keeps failure from your doorstep as well.

This has been my key "fail forward" lesson. Now I'd like to share with you three success stories from direct-sales winners whom I know well and respect with all my heart. They have encountered that devastating failure or that slump or that unexpected brick wall—but instead of letting failure pull them down, they learned the key lessons and worked their way through the challenges to real success and personal satisfaction. Learn from them!

Keith is a man I have known for many years. Our relationship is unique in that we are in agreement about 89 percent of the time. However, when we aren't he is always armed with facts and knowledge of why he believes something different. In ancient times, we would have been mistaken for Sophocles and Aristotle. Keith is a guy who is a giver. He has been there for me both in business, as well as personally, and I count him as a true friend and the voice of reason.

I was introduced to network marketing by a friend of mine, John Richards, who shared a product with me that he thought would benefit me and my wife. Then he proceeded to twist my arm to go to a meeting that was an hour and a half away. That was some 30 years

ago. I'm thankful to that friend for insist-
ing that I look at the business related to that
opportunity.

A little history, looking back after all these
years, he was the only person that ever asked
me to look at a network marketing opportunity. What's odd with that is that over the years
I've known people who've been involved
with MLM, but they never shared it with me
or asked me to look at their opportunity.

Now, there've been others who were
aware I'm involved with MLM and have
approached me, but not a single person who
was not aware of my involvement in network
marketing has ever approached me. The reason is a little further into this story.

At that meeting some 30 years ago I met
Bob Schmidt for the first time. Bob and I went
on to become very good friends. I'll never forget that meeting Bob made a couple points
that changed my life. One, network marketing
allows you to leverage the time and talents of
people who you could never afford to hire
and two, there was a better way than building
a business with all the traditional overhead of
employees such as accounting, shipping and
handling, and so forth. I'll expand on these
points further as well.

The reasons these points were so important is that at that time our family business had

over 100 employees full-time, and during the busy season another 20 to 30 as well. Because of all that is entailed in running a business of that size, his comments caused me to open my mind and consider running a different kind of business. Bob's words caused me to entertain the possibilities of what could be. It's important to revisit those steps. My friend thought enough of me to share the product with us because he thought it would benefit us. Network marketing is built on this principal, sharing a product or service with your family or friends who you think would benefit. Number two, he insisted that I look at the business model of MLM. Reflecting over several decades I think it's important for all of us who are either in network marketing, or considering it, to keep in mind a product or service that you're proud of and want to share with your family and friends. Understanding the business model can help set them free. Maybe it's a retirement, maybe it's a part-time income so they can take a better vacation, maybe it's so they can send their children or grandchildren to a private school. Maybe it's something else entirely. The beauty of MLM is that whatever is important to them, there's a plan with network marketing that will allow them to achieve it.

Now some 30 years later we have business partners in the US, Canada, Mexico, the

Caribbean, South America, and Europe—all because a friend asked me to go to a meeting.

It's important to cover those two-points Bob pointed out to me all those years ago in more detail; first, leveraging the time and talents of people you could never afford to hire.

So, what does that mean, leveraging the time and talents of others? In network marketing, you have business partners who work with you for your success. These are referred to as your up-line, or they may be members of the same company who have been there for many years. These people have a great deal of success, talent, and experience that you're able to tap into for free. Over the years, we've seen very few people take advantage of this talent pool that's available to them. Those who have, however, are the most successful in all of network marketing.

Just for a moment, consider this example of this talent and expertise. Even if you owned the largest hotel in New York City, you would be unable to afford the talent and expertise that I have interviewed in this book. So, the question is, are you availing yourself of the talent in your NM company? They want to help you to succeed!

The second point that Bob pointed out that evening was that within network marketing all the drudgery of owning your own business is shouldered by the company. Some examples are, handling accounting and making sure everybody's paid, processing credit cards, shipping product, as well as research and development. All the resources and expertise a true entrepreneur needs to succeed to create a seamless and well-functioning infrastructure.

Those two points are just as important today, not just for you and your business, but every entrepreneur, as they were to me almost 30 years ago.

So, as you read this book and metabolize it, make it yours. When you're speaking to someone, whether it be family, friends, a coworker, or someone you just met, do them the great favor of making sure you deliver the whole message.

My final thought, after every presentation, do a thorough analysis. Whether that presentation be by phone, in person, or in front of a group, take a few minutes and ask yourself what could I do better next time? And most importantly, don't beat yourself up. Always remember there is a next time. By doing so you will control the controllable; those are the only things you can control. You're not responsible for who's having a bad day.

The best part of network marketing is you get to set the goals.

Chapter 10

THE CONSTANT CHALLENGE

I see myself as an educator. I am committed to a life where learning and improving myself are a constant process. One of the most famous artists in human history, Michelangelo, is renowned for his extraordinary sculptures and paintings. But there's something else he's famous for. In the margin of one of the sketches he completed near the end of his life, he wrote the words, "Ancora imparo," Latin for "I am still learning." A living legend in his own day, the man who painted the ceiling of the Sistine Chapel in Rome, Michelangelo shared his truth that a master of his craft can, and should, stay on the path of life-long learning.

I call this path of lifelong learning the 'constant challenge.' The need to be more, and to do more, is in all of us. My suggestion is that you regularly find new things to learn and do in order to make you feel better about yourself and the direction of your life. Here's an example from one of my recent life experiences.

Although it has little to do with business, my example has everything to do with my personal self-development journey. For many years, off and on, I've competed in several different sports, all somewhat related to martial arts. At age forty-one, with a wife, one child, and more children on the way, I decided that my days of banging heads on mats around the world were pretty much behind me. Although I still roll on mats a few days a week at my buddy Yousef Alirezaei's Jiu jitsu school in Dallas, I put competitive martial arts on the back burner.

Then, while watching the track and field events for the 2008 Summer Olympic Games, I found myself enthralled by the shot put and discus competitions, seeing them with a renewed interest. (I had briefly thrown both way back in my seventh-grade track and field days.) An old discus I had bought for my daughter was gathering dust in the hall closet. Now here's a funny thing, I started lifting weights to get better at throwing. Over time I found I really enjoyed the sport of powerlifting. I started engaging and have been all over the country the last few years at events. Great friendships emerged like the one I mentioned earlier with Dennis Schultz, who is now in our business. Funny how your hobbies can lead to business. I left some blank space here for the following reason. Take some time to think about all the things in life you haven't done yet and list them. However crazy you may think it seems, do it anyway. Your mind engages your body. Then come back and check in a year, 2 years, 5 years and you'll see some of the unimaginable things that you have done!!!

The moral of the story is not about me or my new hobby. My point is that life stays interesting when we take on new challenges—when we push ourselves to reach higher, be stronger, do more, learn more, achieve more, fight more, sweat more, and try harder. Many years ago, I heard about a study claiming that senior-level executives died within a few short years of retirement. The study said that these retired senior execs no longer felt needed in life. Interesting, don't you think?

Find that new reason to get up early or stay up late. Try something you've always wanted to do. Maybe it's playing the guitar, learning to sing, running a 5K, or living your passion. Don't be afraid, no matter what your age, to try a little something new for the first time. The constant challenge makes life vastly more engaging.

Because I am inspired by sayings from leaders who have triumphed in their lives, I want to share some of my favorites. You'll find them throughout the following sections. They are words that I quote often and strive to live by.

Set Your New Personal Record: Citius, Altius, Fortius (Olympic motto)

The happiness of your life depends upon the quality of your thoughts, Take care that you entertain no notions unsuitable to virtue and reasonable nature.

—Marcus Aurelius

In track and field, we describe the drive to constantly do better in your event as setting a new personal record. So, here's my challenge for you: embrace the spirit of lifelong learning and keep moving up to your own next personal record. The chapters of this book pivot around key messages that are crucial to your personal development and the success of your direct-sales business. I've put together a list of resources you can use to take these key messages and keep the momentum of self-development long after finishing this book. Use this list as the foundation for your own as you build the business and the quality of life you want for yourself, your family, and the people who share your professional journey.

Reading should be a regular, consistent activity for anyone who really wants to get ahead in business, as well as in just about every facet of life. I don't know who first coined the expression "All leaders are readers," but I endorse it 1,000 percent.

The lessons of leaders who have worked hard, taken the hits, rebounded, and built renowned and successful businesses are always tremendous sources of knowledge and inspiration. Here are several of my favorites:

- "Ben & Jerry's: The Inside Scoop," by Fred Chico Lager (Crown, 1994)—the story of the building of a customer-friendly and environmentally responsible company that also takes great care of its people.

- "Time to Make the Donuts," by William Rosenberg (Lebhar-Friedman, 2001)—on the building of Dunkin' Donuts, arguably the most famous donut brand in the United States.

- "Where Have All the Leaders Gone?" by Lee Iacocca (Scribner, 2007)—on leadership principles and the current void in the world of politics and business.

- "The Snowball," by Alice Schroeder (Bantam Books, 2008)—about the life and business philosophies of legendary investor Warren Buffett.

- "Harry and Ike," by Steve Neal (Simon & Schuster, 2002)—on the relationship between two great American presidents, Dwight D. Eisenhower and Harry S. Truman.

- "Beyond the Norm," by Norm Miller (Thomas Nelson, 1996)—on the man who has developed Interstate Batteries into a household brand and succeeded in building a network of dealers.

- "The Pampered Chef," by Doris Christopher (Currency Doubleday, 2005)—about the founding and building of a super company that eventually was purchased by Warren Buffett, and containing Doris' secrets to building a $700 million company from her kitchen table.

- "The Starbuck's Experience," by Joseph Michelli (McGraw-Hill, 2007)—as the name suggests, a book all about the amazing journey of Howard Schultz and how he introduced a tiny Seattle roaster to the world.

- "Made in America," by Sam Walton and John Huey (Bantam Books, 1993)—on the building of the world's largest retailer and its founder, Sam Walton, who was a great American and visionary many years before the term visionary was ever used.

- "As a Man Thinketh," by James Allen (written in the latter part of the 1800s and published in 1902)—an early book on the basic idea that what we think about is what we become. It's a short but vital read for anyone wanting to understand the thinking patterns of successful people.

The Value of a Good Mentor

Remember the advice of the "great communicator," Ronald Reagan, in Chapter 1? Finding a good mentor who will invest time and energy in you, teaching you what you need to learn, is more valuable than someone who just hands you a job or a check and walks away. The reason this fact is true is because acquiring important skills is better than "money in the bank."

If you want more financial prosperity and personal satisfaction, your skills are the thing that will get you there. And then you get to pass on the wealth by teaching, challenging, and encouraging the people in your downline.

Here are some of the individuals I consider mentors of mine and who I listen to regularly on audio. Each offers great materials and shares lots of free information via his or her website.

- Tom Peters (www.TomPeters.com). Tom is the best business philosopher in the world. He also gives lots of great, thought-provoking information on his website.

- Zig Ziglar (www.ZigZiglar.com). Zig is one of the greatest sales producers ever. When I listen to Zig, I hear someone who has been a "doer" his entire career.

- Tom Hopkins (www.TomHopkins.com). Tom touched my career early on, and his concept of tie-downs helped to forge my speech pattern and helped me to close thousands of sales.

- Robert Kiyosaki (www.RichDad.com). Robert is a great business teacher/real estate tycoon and has his finger on the pulse of business around the world.

- Jim Rohn (www.JimRohn.com). Jim is a motivator with the ability to make concepts and philosophies come to life.

- Dan Kennedy (www.dankennedy.com). I recommend anything by this author of the NOBS ("no BS") business books. I subscribe to his monthly newsletter, and it's a great value! Dan is perhaps the world's greatest copywriter, and what I love about Dan is that he takes teaching very seriously. I've also used some of his ideas in my advertising with very good results.

I also suggest that you subscribe to the Wall Street Journal, as well as Fortune and Forbes magazines. All are timely and help to keep the mind sharp as you read about who is doing what and what is happening today in business. Even though most of you reading this book are network marketers, at the end of the day, we are all businesspeople.

The more you understand what is happening in the larger context of business and economics, the more you will understand how to create a contemporary rationale for other people to join your business now. Here's a timely example: How about the current economic situation? How long will it last? The bottom line is that everyone needs more money now and for many decades to come, in order to recover from the losses we have and will endure.

I also read the Harvard Business Journal from time to time. The Journal is a solid, well-written read that covers a variety of topics, including management, sales, and marketing.

It Takes Tenacity

Read books, listen to audios, attend seminars—they are the decades of wisdom reduced to invaluable hours.

—Mark Victor Hansen

Making choices is a personal adventure, and not everyone is going to understand or support your choice to build a direct-sales business. As you'll recall, some of my friends and family members thought I was nuts to sell vitamins when I got out of college. The voice I listened to was the voice inside of me, and it made all the difference. I learned that you must stay true to what you believe and have the integrity and belief system to stay the course when others are telling you that you're making a mistake.

Success Magazine offers a wealth of topics that will help you to get more out of your business as well as out your life. It even includes a monthly CD/DVD that features not only today's business leaders but also some of the greats no longer walking the earth. What a privilege to hear Earl Nightingale and Napoleon Hill speaking in their own voices!

Another terrific resource on my list is a company once called Executive Books, and now operating under the name Tremendous Leadership. This company, founded by the late, great Charlie

"Tremendous" Jones, now under the leadership of his daughter, Tracey, has always kept the business classics inexpensive. You can find titles such as "As a Man Thinketh" by James Allen, "Acres of Diamonds" by Russell H. Conwell, and "The Science of Getting Rich" by Wallace D. Wattles in print, eBook, or on audio. I've always believed in the motto, "Turn your car into a classroom." Each month, I make several drives from Dallas to Austin, and I get a chance to refresh my mind with some of these classics, as well as the monthly CD sent by the Dan Kennedy group.

Another motto I believe in is, "When the student is ready, the teacher appears." Why do I (and why should you) listen to audios and watch DVDs of other teachers? The answer is simple: to arouse ideas that are locked in our minds and brought out by others. It constantly amazes me that if I'm searching for an idea, a strategy, a tactic, or just some words for an upcoming speech, I learn just what I need from how someone else presents them.

And finally—there's love. You've got to be asking, why in the world would I mention love here? Well, love is an excellent reason to watch a great movie or read or listen to others' stories. We are not alone. Others have had different, worse, or perhaps similar experiences to our own. Why not gain insights from the lives of others? After all, you'll never live long enough to learn from these mistakes all by yourself. In one of my favorite movies, the character C. S. Lewis (played masterfully by Anthony Hopkins) calls pain God's way to wake up a sleeping world. Learning from others' trials can wake us up to our own journey.

Your Money or Your Life

Wealth is the ability to truly experience life.

—Henry David Thoreau

Sound financial management is the powerful tool essential to both your business and your personal success. Money is also a resource that can be used to bless your life and the lives of others—whether it's setting up a college fund for your kids, giving 10 percent of your income to your church, or making an annual donation to an international human relief organization.

It is said that Einstein called compound interest the most powerful force in the universe. Whether or not he actually uttered those words, the truth is that compound interest and other financial functions remain a mystery to far too many people today—especially entrepreneurial businesspeople like us. If you've allowed money management to go unexplained in your world or to be something that those "financial types" handle, it's time for a new attitude. Learn about the power of money. It will enhance your life, as well as the lives of your loved ones and the people in your business.

Before we move into resources on money, what is money anyway? It's a mixture of paper and power.

If you were stranded on a mountaintop, about to freeze to death, and you had $10 million in cash in a brown paper bag, the money wouldn't get you off the mountain, would it? However, with a book of matches and a few pieces of wood, perhaps you could build a fire and burn the cash to stay warm and send a signal to be seen by a passing pilot.

Hopefully, all of you reading this are not freezing on top of a mountain. However, the decisions you are making now will affect the balance of your life. For better or worse, money—or the lack of it—will determine everything from your healthcare to how you spend your time and who you can bless with it or choose not to bless with it. Does your church need some new hymnals? Does a local elderly person need a donation for new eyeglasses or a wheelchair? These simple examples are ones we'd all love to help with, but do we have the money to do so?

We can if we understand that there is abundance available all over the earth and that this abundance is ours if we learn the skills to acquire it. The marketplace allows for all we can earn if our skills meet the proper opportunity and are supported by hard work and dedication to a singular goal.

Here's a basic formula on monetary distribution that has served me well:

- 10 percent to charity
- 30 percent to taxes
- 30 percent to business building

- 20 percent to overhead

- 10 percent put away for the future

Does it always work out exactly this way? Pretty much so. Here, too, are a few of my credos for you to consider:

Render unto Caesar the things that are Caesar's. In modern terms, make sure that you put away at least 30 percent of your earnings for the taxman. He will collect either way, so why not pay him on time and save the interest and penalties. As an independent small-business owner, you are given much freedom, as well as the ability to maximize tax savings. However, the taxman (Caesar) expects his cut. Don't think, like a few direct sellers, that you are going to earn a fortune and not pay your taxes. While I am for small government and low taxes, our job is not to fight city hall. Our job is to create wealth and opportunity for ourselves and our team.

Keeping up with the Joneses. Why even do this? The only person you need to impress is your CPA. You can live without the latest car or gadget. Put your money into your business, and don't live beyond your means. Buy good used cars (especially the luxury kind), and let the original owner pay the high luxury tax, if applicable. The same rationale applies to your home. Be practical because you don't need the burden of extra overhead such as high utility costs or real estate taxes. Save your money for a rainy day or, better yet, to promote your business.

Finally, here are three resources that I recommend:

Investor's Business Daily: I enjoy reading this valuable money tool, which gives lots of facts and figures as well as a daily interview with a great entrepreneur. It's inspiring to read how other people have built their fortunes.

CNBC or Bloomberg: Listen daily to know what is happening in the greater business market. Everything affects everything else. That being the case, even though you are focused on MLM as a business, it helps to know what is going on in the macro business world.

"Rich Dad, Poor Dad: What the Rich Teach Their Kids About Money—That the Poor and Middle Class Do Not!" by Robert Kiyosaki (Grand Central Publishing, 1998). This is the book where Kiyosaki gave the world his "cashflow quadrants," which clearly illustrate the dynamics of moving from someone who works for a paycheck to a person who generates wealth through passive income—which is exactly what direct sales offers.

A Fair Day's Work for Long-Term Rewards

Management works in the system; leadership works on the system.

—Steven Covey

In Chapter 4 you learned that a daily method of operation (DMO) is necessary for building a successful business. This action plan serves the unique needs of a direct-sales business, spelling out the value-added tasks that you perform on a day-by-day basis. In network marketing, there's no such thing as an hourly wage. You get paid for results, no matter how long it takes to get them.

First, here are a few ideas for building a good DMO:

- Get in the habit of working consistent hours in your business. For example, I usually start each day with a good workout, and by 10:00 a.m., I'm at my desk, working throughout the day until I quit for dinner around 5:00 p.m. Then I spend a couple hours with my kids and share in their activities. At 7:00 p.m., I normally return to the phone and make calls until 10:00 p.m. I also work Saturday afternoon for three to four hours. Sunday is a day of rest and all about family time. I might make a few calls in the late afternoon, if necessary, but otherwise, I honor the Sabbath.

- It's not so much about the hours; it's about the value of what you do during those hours. Dedicate your time to doing what is necessary to build your business, which means making the calls, marketing your business, meeting new prospects, and supporting your people. I end each workday knowing what I will accomplish the next day, and most of my time revolves around spending time in the field—in person, on the phone, or online—to grow my business.

We talked about your sales efforts and how the money you want to make drives the number of sales interactions you need to earn that money. If your DMO tells you that you have to get in front of ten people a day to get the money you need, then it's up to you to schedule those calls or show up ready to network at those business events. Bear in mind that there is no better teacher in direct sales than actually doing the selling yourself. You can read all the books, listen to all the tapes, and go to all the seminars, but if you don't get in front of as many people as possible, you will be wasting your time. If given a choice about how to spend their time, all the champion-level network marketing leaders I've known would choose to spend their time in the field.

That said, we also can learn from the sales masters in our business and the business greats in other industries. Joe Girard (auto sales) and Joe Gandolfo (insurance sales) are perhaps the two greatest salesmen ever in their industries. They both have amazing concepts that make sense for anyone trying to sell anything—or just deal with human beings. While I never had a chance to meet either man, they have both inspired me with their lives, accomplishments, and ideas.

- "How to Sell Anything to Anybody," by Joe Girard (Grand Central, 1986)—the best book on sales technique, hands down. It's a true classic.

- "How to Make Big Money Selling," by Joe Gandolfo (HarperCollins, 1985)—another must-read book about making money through sales.

Moving up to the next level—from good to great—means that your company must have a crucially important point of difference. It's all about having the right people on the bus—the right people running sales, marketing, and finance, as well as all matters of leadership. Learn more by reading this terrific book on growing a strong, vital business:

- "Good to Great: Why Some Companies Make the Leap and Others Don't," by Jim Collins (HarperCollins, 2001)—studies why some companies become huge while others just exist.

- "More than a Pink Cadillac," by Jim Underwood (McGraw-Hill, 2003)—on the incredible nine leadership principles endorsed by Mary Kay.

Finally, let's look at time management. The first-time management technique I used, which came from many sources, was to write down and prioritize the six most important things to do the next day—before going to sleep. This practice still works well for me today. There also have been many fine books written on time management, including "Do

It Tomorrow," by Mark Forster (Hodder, 2006). Forster also has a great blog about managing time.

Putting Your Best Face Forward

Here's a little advice I received many years ago from the legendary Tom Hopkins. I was a shy young man, and one day I went to see Tom speak in New York. I found the guts to approach him, and he gave me a great strategy: *Do what you fear most!* As a matter of fact, Tom wrote it on the back of his business card and I still have it in my business archives. Amazing how good concepts are timeless.

If you have some apprehension about presenting to a group, Hopkins' valuable lesson can be your guide and motivation. I've always believed that I knew more than the audience in front of me. Tell your audience what you know. Keep to the facts of your company (who you are), your product (what it does), and the earning opportunity (how will they get paid). Remember, most people show up because they have a legitimate interest in finding a product and a financial opportunity—so tell them what you know.

Network marketing's primary sales vehicle remains the meeting. Whether you're gathering a few members of your downline in your living room, getting to know a new prospect and her husband over coffee at Starbucks, or speaking to a crowd of hundreds of people in a hotel ballroom, the meeting is where you're responsible for presenting your key messages with confidence, clarity, and the goal of enriching the lives of the people there to listen to you.

Let's start with some recommendations for the basics: how to improve your public speaking skills, from putting together a good presentation to speaking to a crowd.

One of the people whose materials I studied was the great Bill Gove. If you want to improve your speaking skills, any of Gove's writings or seminars is terrific. Many of today's leading speakers were trained using Gove's principles and tools. You can learn more at *www.speechworkshop.com*. Another great group is Toastmasters Anonymous, which has helped people to improve their public speaking skills for years.

Of course, the best way to learn how to give a good speech is to speak in public as often as you can. Volunteer to speak for free at local groups. There are always audiences looking for information and to be entertained. Find out beforehand the rules of the group to which you'll be speaking. Many groups don't allow you to sell to them. However, by volunteering to give a free speech on a topic with which you are familiar, you can always make contacts to use at a later point.

As far as speechwriting is concerned, there are many books to recommend, of course. When I write a speech, I normally use broad strokes as far as my subjects. For example, I have four or five main topics to discuss, and then I make footnotes under each. Here's a topic example:

Main topic: How to build an international downline:

- Work local with ethnic groups from the country we'll be opening.
- Contact the Chamber of Commerce for that group, if one exists.
- Check out available media in the market for ad placement.
- See if there are any networking groups in your city that meet on a regular basis where you could visit, perhaps give product samples, etc.

Here are a couple of my favorite books on speechwriting that include examples from the masters:

- "Lend Me Your Ears: Great Speeches in History," by William Safire (Cobbett Corporation, 1992)—also has many classic speeches for your education and entertainment.
- "I Got to Tell You: Speeches of Lee Iacocca," by Lee Iacocca and Matthew W. Seeger (Wayne State University Press, 1994)—a collection of the extraordinary speeches given by Lee Iacocca.

We also learned about a variety of meeting formats in this business, including how to best plan and run a two-on-one meeting. For more insight on two-on-one meetings, I recommend:

- "Big Al Tells All: The Recruiting System (Sponsoring Magic)," by Tom Schreiter (Kass, 1985)—a must-have book that takes the reader back to the basics of network marketing. Schreiter describes how the two-on-one presentation technique is still the most powerful results-generating method you can use to sign up new recruits.

Train to Gain

A network marketing business that is worth your investment of time and talent is one that has earned real bragging rights about how well it trains its people. No matter what product or service a company offers, people in a downline will only be as good as the upline leaders who are training them. As an upline person, you have the responsibility to be a teacher, coach, and mentor to your downline folks—especially distributors who are new to your business. This means that you, as a leader, have to be ready to teach, refine, and support the skills of your team. You have to be dedicated and passionate about training.

Here are a few additional points on running training sessions:

- Keep everything about your messages at about an eighth-grade reading level. You don't need to impress people with fancy words or a big vocabulary. Remember: If they can't do it or say it, they can't duplicate it.

- Realize that most people are visual, so use examples that are visual. Here's an example of what I use: Let's say that your pay plan pays eight levels. To make this visually clear and simple for your audience, start by asking one person in the front row to stand up. Ask his or her name (let's say that it's Tom). You tell the audience that whatever Tom sells, you make 5 percent on it. Let's say that Tom sells $1,000 this month, and you earn $50 on Tom's sales. Then ask the person seated behind Tom to stand up. We'll call her Mary. Mary sells $2,000 this month. You make 5 percent or $100. Do this using a few more people in the room, and everyone gets the idea!

- If it can't be duplicated, it won't work. The ideas and exercises you suggest must be able to be done immediately by everyone in the room. If they can't see themselves doing it, they won't duplicate it anywhere else either.

- Teach people to employ themselves. The more skills you can give your people that help them to see ink strikes on paper, the better it is for everyone.

- As Joe Gandolfo has always said, selling is 98 percent about understanding human beings and 2 percent about product knowledge. While it's important for your people to have in-depth knowledge of your product or service, great sales results will depend more on knowing and understanding what speaks to the human being standing in front of you.

Stand Out from the Crowd

You don't get in life what you want. You get what you are.

—Les Brown

All the special elements that set you, your product or service, and your company, apart from the rest of the marketing noise out in the world are your points of difference. When it comes to building a brand, I've found it highly worthwhile to read books that chronicle the path of a brand from its birth to its global reach.

For learning how other companies have used their brand's points of difference to reap international recognition, here are two books to add to your list:

- "The Tipping Point: How Little Things Can Make a Big Difference," by Malcolm Gladwell (Little, Brown, 2000)—reveals how items such as cell phones and DVD players have become household words.

- "Pour Your Heart Into It: How Starbucks Built a Company One Cup at a Time," by Howard Schultz and Dori Jones Yang (Hyperion, 1999)—on some of the techniques and ideas that Schultz has used to grow the Starbucks brand.

Mastering Low-Cost Marketing

For those of us determined to grow our network marketing business, marketing becomes quite simply—and literally—a way of life. Every trip to the store, every group we join, and every person we meet is an opportunity to market our business. This is easy when you see every encounter as a chance to present a new contact with products or services that will enhance his or her quality of life or to build financial freedom in this last bastion of free enterprise.

- "Food for Thought," by Phil Romano (Dearborn, 2005)—written by the creator of Fuddruckers, Romano's, Macaroni Grill, and other themed restaurants, and providing great insight on how to be creative and profitable in business.

If you were to poll most people about marketing, they'd probably talk about newspaper ads and brochures. Neither of those tactics is wrong, but guerilla marketing offers you much more than ad space and handouts. The "father of guerilla marketing" is author and lecturer Jay Conrad Levinson. Levinson offers many different resources on guerilla marketing—including a free weekly e-newsletter that offers simple, nontraditional, and effective tips for building a business. Sign up for it at *www.gmarketing.com*.

Online and on the Money

Network marketing is all about personal, face-to-face time with your customers, prospects, and downline people. But we also know that the internet has made virtually the whole world accessible to those running a network marketing business. To use the internet effectively means knowing how to create a warm, welcoming environment through an impersonal electronic medium. Some people do this well. However, internet marketing has its own set of skills, and the internet arena seems to evolve overnight. For example, Facebook and Twitter are transforming how people do business today, and new social media sites will have been launched by the time you read this book. If you've decided to tread slowly into doing business online, never fear—there are people ready to help you.

Never Give Up

Don't be afraid to fail.

When my neighbor's dad gave me this advice back in the late 1970s, I didn't really know what he meant. When you're seventeen years old, you don't know what much means, but today at fifty-eight, I can tell you what he meant clearly: you only get ahead in life by occasionally getting your nose bloodied.

This was crystal clear in contact sports from early on. In business, the message is sometimes not as easy to discern right away, and you need a few years to figure it out.

However, the bottom line is that you need to constantly test your strategy and tactics. Sometimes you need to lose some money to figure out what not to do. Regardless, you will be way ahead of those weak-kneed individuals who won't even try for fear of failing every once in a while.

Take baseball as an example. A good player at the highest level has a batting average of about .300 and, in a perfect world, he could bat 1000. What this means is that he fails seven out of ten times at bat. Last time I looked, major leaguers at the .300 level earn millions of dollars annually. Isn't it interesting that we get in business and are terrified to fail?

In our business, we get paid for talking to people. What if we only sponsored three out of ten? What if we did it five days a week? Each of us would be amazingly successful. The results we get, we get paid for, and just like the .300 hitter, the more we fail, the more we succeed. Throughout all my years of trial and error, I've maintained the mind-set that failure is a valuable teaching tool. You just need to learn the fine art of failing forward. Analyze what you've done wrong or what your gut says you could have done better and adjust your course for next time.

I'm obviously a big sports fan and a passionate collector of personal stories in which an individual has turned failure into victory. Bookstores have lined their shelves with biographies of men and women who overcame the most daunting of odds, often when others were sure they would fail. We can learn from these heroes. It doesn't mean that every step you take with your direct-sales business needs to be heroic. But you do need to call on something heroic in you to move up in spite of a misstep or outright business disaster.

The skill to fail forward is another vital lesson you can share with your downline, and it is an invaluable key learning for your children. Here are some of my favorite books on failing forward:

- "The Power of Positive Thinking," by Dr. Norman Vincent Peale (Prentice-Hall, 1952)—the first book I ever read on personal growth, which I read at age seventeen when I was recovering from spinal surgery. Dr. Peale talks about how to handle real world problems.

- "What Losing Taught Me About Winning," by Fran Tarkenton and Wes Smith (Simon and Schuster, 1997)—Fran's small-business strategies have helped me in my businesses countless times.

Support from Our Industry

Of course, the network marketing industry itself provides e-magazines and organizations that offer valuable information and recommendations for building, and sustaining, a thriving direct-sales business. Articles, helpful hints, and success stories all can serve to inspire you and your downline as you strategize for success daily. One of the websites I suggest is *www.DSA.org*, which offers lots of information, statistics, and insights about the direct-selling industry. There is much to be learned from this site! I also recommend *www.DSWA.org*, which provides helpful information for women who are seeking success in our industry. This website offers great training programs and information about local chapters to aid in the growth of your business.

It's Time to Move Up

The resources I've shared with you in this chapter are the tip of the iceberg. My list grows on a constant basis, and I share what I learn with my downline team. If you haven't already started your own "learning library," beginning one is an action step I highly recommend—and one that you can use to inspire your own downline.

So, you're ready to start a direct-sales business, or to take your direct-sales business to the next level, armed with the hard-earned lessons I've shared in this book and the willingness to accept the constant challenge of learning about yourself and what matters to you. I started this book with my own story—how an open-minded college grad took the risk to follow a business opportunity that people in his world found hard to understand. The choice I made then, and the choices I make every day to fuel my businesses and bless my life and the people in it, have made all the difference.

Today, my businesses span the globe. I wake up each morning grateful for the opportunities I get to work with great people of integrity—from the full-time business owners, like me, to the micro-entrepreneurs who run their direct-sales businesses on the weekends. We're all connected by a common passion, an eagerness to succeed, the willingness to go the distance, and the drive to make a difference in this world—even if we have to get a little banged up from time to time.

I tell my people the direct-sales industry is where you can really do something with your life. This last bastion of free enterprise is where average people like you and me can achieve greatness. And this is especially true during a questionable economic climate. We all know that the downturn eventually will swing back up. Meanwhile, the time is now for establishing multiple sources of income. There is no better time to build a financial fortress around you and your loved ones, a fortress that no economic downturn, no crazy tax code, nor any outside circumstance—be it an illness, lawsuit, or even the death of a loved one—can destroy.

So, as I close this book as the year 2020 looms and begins, I have a few thoughts—some personal and some for us all. This is the end of the "Moving Up" series that I started way back in 2005 with our first edition. When I wrote that first book I didn't know I could do it. Like most things in life you find it in yourself to do things you didn't realize you could do. How many people have used that book as guidance toward growing their business? How many lives can I hope that we helped to improve with the concepts and message way back then. On a personal level, my kids were in diapers and grade school. Now, Camille is an adult, Fred and Grace are being educated at a great prep school, and Fred is starting to look at college options. Where did the years go? That said, what about you?

If you read those words back in 2005, did you move up in your life? In your business? How about if you read the second edition in 2011? If not, the good news is that it's never too late to move up. Don't stop yourself with negative thoughts or self-doubts, although we all have some from time to time. One of my mentors, the late, great Jim Rohn, had a speech about seed, soil, sunshine, rain, and miracle of life. I had the honor of having lunch with Jim in Dallas many years ago. He was a great man. Many times I think about those simple yet life-giving elements that Jim spoke of and ask myself what have I done with them? Well, part of writing to help others is we do so to most help the person in the mirror. So, I'm off to continue my life path of Moving Up. I hope you'll do the same.

John Solleder has written "Moving Up: Real Life Secrets for Getting from Here to There" (Volume 1, 2005, volume 2, 2011). He has also been a featured writer in several Networking Times articles. Watch for his next title "Leave Nothing to Chance" with co-author Foster Owusu, coming in June 2020.

He welcomes your contact through his facebook fan page, "John Moving Up Solleder".